American Deserters in Sweden

AMERICAN DESERTERS IN SWEDEN

The Men and Their Challenge

by THOMAS LEE HAYES

Association Press/New York

AMERICAN DESERTERS IN SWEDEN

Copyright © 1971 by Thomas Lee Hayes

———

Association Press, 291 Broadway, New York, N.Y. 10007

Standard Book Number: 8096-1817-6

Library of Congress Catalog Card Number: 75-152890

PRINTED IN THE UNITED STATES OF AMERICA

For Bob, and Greg, and Jerry,
and all the victims of this war.

Contents

Preface

By mid-1970 some young American was going "over the hill" every three minutes from the United States Army. Somebody's son was "splitting for good," deserting the United States armed forces, every ten minutes. More than 89,000 men were absent without leave from duty related to the Vietnam War for more than thirty days in one year alone (fiscal 1970.)

This book is about our experience—my own, with my wife and our two daughters—with several hundred of these men. The place was Sweden, where these men have gone to seek asylum from military service in Vietnam and from the tyranny of the military as they experienced it. With the deserters are a much smaller number of draft resisters or dodgers, many of whom we came to know as well.

Theirs is a cause, an insistent claim that sends their mother country, if popular opinion is to be believed, "up against the wall." Most Americans can grant that a man might be conscientiously opposed to killing. Yet these same Americans believe that once a man has entered military service the door to objection is closed, that a young man must store his conscience in the attic along with his civilian clothes. I shall try to show that it is very difficult to do that, even when you try hard.

When the costs of the war in Vietnam are tallied, we will all remember the lives lost there. More than 50,000 American lives; more than two million Vietnamese dead; countless wounded on both sides; countless numbers imprisoned and tortured.

Yet there are other costs. To America, there is the cost of a crisis in the nation's conscience over the goals and means of

America's war policies; the massive inflation caused by the more than 120 billion dollars spent on the war; the enervating effect upon programs and workers throughout the society; and the enormous drain out of the country of those driven to choose exile or prison rather than participation in the American war machine.

These men, their girl friends and their wives, were the members in our parish out of bounds, over the hill without the permission of the United States government. Although this book is about these men and women, it cannot speak for them. They do this with their own lives far better than I can do with my words. The book is a reflection of my own experience. It is designed as a kind of contemporary act of reflection, in the belief that there is something of the contemplative in each of us. I hope the reader will enter into dialogue with me and with himself and come to his own conclusions. If the effort challenges some to an entirely different outlook toward these men, I shall be especially gratified. If it upsets some others without changing their minds, I shall still be pleased, though I hope not without compassion. But if, out of any reader's own meditation, the book brings some en-joy-ment, a liberating hold on the roots of the human struggle common to all of us, I shall find my purpose fulfilled. In any case, I write because I found that I had to. "I love to tell the story."

Years ago, I attended the Brattle Street Theater in Cambridge, Massachusetts, for a showing of the old film, *The House of Rothschild*. On the way out, a little old lady was savoring the roots of her Jewish heritage. She kept murmuring to herself, "Thank God, they're still telling that story." Long after the war in Vietnam is ended, we shall be speaking of those who resisted this war and paid a price for doing so. I believe that those who did will be in the honor guard of our nation's conscience as long as we exist as a people. They will take their tour of duty as men of honor, fulfilling the prophecy of the late John F. Kennedy that we shall not have peace until that day when the conscientious objector is as honored as the veteran is now.

For her work in typing much of the manuscript I wish to

thank Miss Virginia Cook; for a fine association, good friendship and also reading of the manuscript in its early stages, I thank James Walch; for conceiving the project and supporting me clearly throughout I thank Clergy and Laymen Concerned, especially the organization's executive secretary, my friend, Richard R. Fernandez; for his belief in me and in the importance of the story I thank my editor, Robert Wright; for her very special insight and comfort when we needed it much I thank Mrs. Beatrice Seitzman; for more than 1,000 extra meals, for putting up some 400 overnight guests, for her extraordinary largeness of spirit under continuous stress I thank my wife, Janet; for friendliness shown toward the men and understanding toward me I thank our daughters, Sharon and Jennifer; and finally, for the gift of themselves, I thank the men and women who with all their own struggles took time to befriend us.

It should be clear that without the support and interest of its people, the Swedish government could not have been moved to grant our men the right to come and remain there. To those who went out of their way to make our work possible, among them members of the Swedish Vietnam Committee and the Swedish churches, I dare to extend on behalf of millions of Americans our fraternal gratitude.

I hope, then, that many people will believe me and understand me when I say that this work was so great a privilege that if I do nothing else with my life than work among these young Americans, in exile because of America's war in Southeast Asia, my life will have been worth living.

September 1, 1970   T.L.H.

American Deserters in Sweden

chapter 1

YOSSARIAN LIVES

Yossarian laughed with buoyant scorn and shook his head. "I'm not running *away* from my responsibilities, I'm running *to* them. There's nothing negative about running away to save my life. You know who the escapists are, don't you, Danby? Not me and Orr."

"Chaplain, please talk to him, will you? He's deserting. He wants to run away to Sweden."

"Wonderful!" cheered the chaplain, proudly throwing on the bed a pillowcase full of Yossarian's clothing. "Run away to Sweden, Yossarian. And I'll stay here and persevere."

—Joseph Heller, *Catch-22*

Yossarian lives. I found him in Sweden when I got there in 1969. You remember Yossarian. He's the World War II combat pilot, veteran of seventy missions, and anti-hero of Joseph Heller's novel, *Catch-22*, now made into a movie. When Heller's novel came out, the readers and the critics all thought it comic but absurd. Now a lot of folk find it madly prophetic.

American deserters from the Vietnam war in Sweden. Sweden —what an unlikely place for American political refugees! A country the size of the state of California but, with 8,000,000 persons, less than half that state's population. The Land of the Midnight Sun and the Winter Light. And since 1967 the haven for young Americans seeking asylum from participation in the Vietnam war.

Who are these young Yossarians? Where did they come from?

And why Sweden, of all places? These are some of the questions I posed for myself as my wife, our two daughters and I set about to serve in our parish out of bounds. The answers we found were both surprising and familiar.

We learned that the first American deserters arrived in the summer of 1967, and made it unheralded. They were two: Ray Jones,* of Detroit, Michigan, who later turned himself in to U.S. military authorities and yet returned to Sweden with his wife and two children; and Michael Haire, of Beaufort, South Carolina, who came to Sweden via England where he had fled from duty in Bad Kreuznach, Germany, after two and one-half years in the U.S. Army. But few knew of the actions of Jones and Haire, or of the many others who were already deserting from U.S. forces in 1967, until the unprecedented publicity that surrounded the desertion of the "Intrepid Four."

"Four Patriotic Deserters"

On October 23, 1967, in a Tokyo coffee house, four American sailors agreed not to return to their ship, an aircraft carrier, the U.S.S. *Intrepid.* The four were Craig W. Anderson of San Jose, California; Richard D. Bailey, of Jacksonville, Florida; John Michael Barilla of Catonsville, Maryland; and Michael A. Lindner of Mount Pocono, Pennsylvania. They were deeply upset about the war and their participation in it. They were fed up with the military system required to prosecute the war. And they decided they would not return to active duty in the Tonkin Gulf in support of the planes bombing North Vietnam at the time.

Three years later, Craig, Rick, John and Mike were still in Sweden. I met and talked with all four of the men. Craig is married now to a Swedish girl, Eva, and they have a son, Paul. Rick was working in a lumber camp, the last I heard. John was in school and into some heavy meditation, and Mike was doing

---

* In all cases, an individual's right to privacy has been respected by use of a fictitious identity unless specific permission to use the correct name has been granted.

odd jobs, enough to survive. The most remarkable thing they have in common is that they see themselves as rather ordinary fellows. They are straightforward in manner and serious about putting together a new life in exile in Sweden.

What was important at the time was that their action was extraordinary. No one had ever announced his act of desertion, not publicly at least. Generally, desertion was not an action to be proud of. Yet there they were, the four of them, in a press conference in Tokyo, November 1, 1967. They read a joint statement:

You are looking at four deserters, four patriotic deserters from the United States armed forces. Throughout history, the name deserter has applied to cowards, traitors and misfits. We are not concerned with categories or labels. We have reached the point where we must stand up for what we believe to be the truth.

This overshadows the consequences imposed by the categories.

Why have we done this?

We oppose the escalation of the Vietnam war because in our opinion the murder and needless slaughter of civilians through the systematic bombing of an agricultural, poverty-stricken country by a technological society is criminal.

We believe that the United States must discontinue all bombing and pull out of Vietnam, letting the Vietnamese people govern themselves.

We believe that a majority of the people in Japan and the United States oppose the war in Vietnam, but are individually indifferent in taking actions to move toward peace. We appeal to the people of the world to realize that each one of us is responsible for the slaughter in Vietnam.

We believe that further escalation in Vietnam will eventually lead to a direct confrontation with China, resulting in a world war.

We oppose the war as true Americans, not affiliated with any political party.

We face military disciplinary action as a result of our beliefs, therefore we seek political asylum in Japan or any other country not involved in the war.

We believe that the people in Japan seeking peace in Vietnam should unite with the Americans and all other peaceful people of the world in a united stand against the war.

We oppose the militaristic impression the United States is forcing on the world. Through military occupation and economic domination, the United States controls many small countries.

We oppose the American military forces in Vietnam, but not Americans. With only 7 per cent of the world's population and control of one-third of the world's wealth, Americans should make a humanitarian stand in Vietnam rather than a military stand.

We believe that all military expenses should be cut. The money now spent for the war effort should be rechanneled into health, education and welfare throughout the world.

It is our fervent hope that our actions will move *you*, wherever you are, whoever you are, to stand up and do whatever you can to bring peace to Vietnam.

To conclude, we think that we have made it clear that our decision to publicize our action in deserting from the military has been made in the hope that other Americans—particularly those in the military—the people of Japan and of all countries can be spurred into action to work toward stopping this war.

We appeal to all of you wherever you may be to take action in in whatever way you can to bring peace to the troubled country of Vietnam. Let all of us unite together and work for peace.

John Michael Barilla
Richard D. Bailey
Michael A. Lindner
Craig W. Anderson

One of the obvious factors in this statement is its political content: these men abhor the war precisely because they are Americans and find themselves responsible for the prosecution of the war. The same theme of motivation comes up time and again in talking with the American deserters and, indeed, is reflected in individual statements the four made at the time.

"I am just an American . . ."

John's father was a rigger for Bethlehem Steel in Baltimore. John enlisted in the Navy after high school. Faced with the draft and unable to see himself as a college man, he went the route of better than 80 per cent of our armed forces: he was "recruited." "All war is ugly and Vietnam is no exception," he said. "I cannot understand how the United States, supposedly standing for a world peace, could possibly release such a colossal destructive force against a small underdeveloped Asian country. One of my strongest feelings against the Vietnamese conflict is that no one seems to have a reasonable argument for it." Mindful of the reaction of many Americans, John added, "By some I will be labeled as an anti-American or a Communist. These are just emotive words again and none of them actually apply to me. I am just an American standing up for what I think is right, and I'm not alone."

I don't know what Mike's father does, but Mike comes from an average middle-class family of one married sister and one brother in college. Mike decided to "desert the military and the crimes it represents." He felt strongly that he had no political affiliation, and has none today to my knowledge, yet he reasoned, "I don't feel that I was there [Tonkin Gulf] doing something for the land or the people of America, which and whom I love in the same way the Vietnamese love their land and their people (what's left of them)." Voicing a theme found among many GI's today, Lindner spoke of "what I believe in and stand up for—these things that are guaranteed me by the Bill of Rights and denied me by the military."

(All four men considered their chances of gaining conscientious objector status within the military so hopeless as to be laughable. That they were probably correct is corroborated by the figures of the Department of the Navy for 1967. The rate of discharge for conscientious objection to war for that period was 19 per cent. Of the 105 applications made, only twenty were approved. None of these were granted from a "war zone," for example, Vietnam.)

Craig expected to complete his college studies and to become a law-enforcement officer. He had been in the U.S. Naval Air Reserves, doing a six-year hitch. During the first six months he made it to only one reserves meeting and found himself in a psychological and moral bind. After consulting a civilian psychologist he tried for a discharge as being psychologically unfit. He refused to wear his uniform on July 1, 1966, at the Alameda Naval Air Station and was placed on report for disobedience of a direct order. He later agreed to wear the uniform and shortly afterward was interviewed by a naval psychiatrist. The doctor recommended Anderson's discharge, but the captain overruled him and Anderson was assigned to active duty. Anderson himself admits he had "a clear disciplinary record for the year and three months" he served. After observing the "tons and tons of bombs loaded and jet after jet launched" from the *Intrepid*, he decided to desert. In his statement, he appealed "to the youth of America as a fellow young American to stop the war machine." Craig Anderson thought he must do his part in stopping "the Green Machine," as many GI's call it.

Rick Bailey was probably a "heavy" from the standpoint of knowledge about the military and about the war itself. He comes from a military family; his father is a former pilot and commander in the Naval Reserves. His prepared statement was twice the length of the others, and those of us who know Rick can understand why. He said he was no expert, but he dealt at some length, and intelligently, with the Communist label he imagined would be stuck on him. He had joined the Navy, but he called it "the recruiting poster Navy." He charged that warring in Vietnam was "only an excuse, and a horrible one" for "the real objective—China." He reasoned that "to understand our stand, [people] will have to take a look at the entire United States system and their stand, and make an unbiased decision." "The United States government and people," he said, "have become so involved with 'the system' that human values and feelings involved have become secondary." And he concluded, "I am an American. It hurts to leave my friends, family and future there, knowing I can never return. But I am willing to do this and *be* labeled a Communist, if this is what it takes to stop the war and bring America to its senses. Let the *spirit* of the Constitution prevail."

But Why Sweden?

Some 500 men have followed the Intrepid Four to Sweden. Relatively few, perhaps twenty, went the same route, via the assistance of Beheiren, the Japanese Peace Committee, and through the Soviet Union. In all, there are perhaps fifty men there who deserted from Vietnam. Still they come at a rate of better than one a day, double that in the summer months. And in Canada, open to American deserters since May, 1969, many times that come every day. The Canadian government does not keep figures on the military or selective service histories of Americans who seek "landed immigrant" status there. Support groups, however, estimate that the figure for draft-age Americans in Canada approaches 80,000, or one per cent of the Canadian population. About 10,000 of these are said to be former U.S. military personnel. With so large a number going to Canada, how, then, did Sweden's acceptance of 500 or so become critical?

It is commonly reported that in 1967, 83 per cent of Swedish public opinion was opposed to the war. When the Swedish government permitted our men to apply for political asylum—a status the men do *not* receive; they are granted a "right to stay" —it was a policy consistent with its foreign policy of opposition to the U.S. prosecution of the war in Vietnam. Generally, I found that the Swedes thought U.S. involvement in the war was "stupid" rather than "immoral," though they have been revolted by its inhumanity along with much of world opinion. Sweden also had a precedent from the mid-fifties when it granted asylum to some objectors to the French war in Algeria. Still, a decade later, why Sweden?

Not being either a member of the North Atlantic Treaty Organization or of the Warsaw Pact, Sweden sees itself as a neutral social democracy. In the period from 1930 to 1970, Sweden became one of the most successful countries in the world as measured by the pace and quality of its industrialization. Politically and economically, Sweden sees her society as a bridge between the socialist and the capitalist countries of Europe. About 90 per cent of its wealth is privately owned, much of it by only fifteen families. Another 5 per cent has been nationalized, and the remainder is held by cooperatives.

Because Sweden was technically neutral during World War II, its policies then were suspect as "hustling on both sides of the street." Germans who sought refuge from Nazism in Sweden during the war were returned in some cases after the war, a policy that resulted in the prosecution of some of those refugees. Yet in the postwar period, especially within the last fifteen years, more than 500,000 emigrants from many countries around the world have sought a home in Sweden. This means that one of every sixteen persons now living on Swedish soil is a foreigner, a fact that has cut deeply into traditional Swedish isolation.

I saw at least part of Sweden's policy in regard to the American Vietnam war objectors as an effort to atone for whatever national guilt they may have experienced for a false neutrality in the past. Swedish opposition to the Vietnam war and the Swedes' support of our young Americans was a way of saying, *på Svenska*, "Never again." The forging of a new political integrity in the modern world by a country thrust into economic and political prominence in less than a generation seems to be part of the answer to why it was Sweden that became home away from home for many.

Dropping Your Pants in Public

In 1968, levies for Vietnam were coming down steadily on American bases in Germany. The manpower pool for combat-ready status stood at a half-million men. As those orders came down, the men had to decide. Not to decide was to decide anyway. They knew that all too soon they would be in Vietnam, and they would find no hiding place there. Trained as soldiers, they knew it came down to "kill or be killed" and "follow orders if you want to get out of there alive." So Johnnie began dropping his gun and telling others about it. It was like dropping your pants in public. And it was embarrassing to the United States government and to the brass, whose "property" these men officially were.

"Who are these guys, anyway?" I have often been asked. One way to answer this question is to tell you where they hail from originally in the States.

Joe comes from St. Paul, Minnesota, and Charlie's from Lewisburg, Tennessee; Bill's from St. Louis; Buz comes from Braintree, Massachusetts; Walter's from around Boston; Justin comes from Redding, California; Rich from Chesnee, South Carolina; Dick is from Denver; Gerry's from Westmont, New Jersey; Willie from Cheyenne, Oklahoma; Rod from Lincoln, Nebraska; Kim from Boise, Idaho; Max from outside Jackson, Mississippi; Frank from Macon, Georgia; Charlie from Helena, Montana; Mike from Alaska; Rich from Honolulu; Herb from outside Tacoma; Steve from Brazil, Indiana; Ed from Derry, Pennsylvania; and Mike from Tobyhanna, Pennsylvania. And on and on.

You can surely get the idea. Call it a litany of origins. Smaller cities and towns. These men are the decidedly unsilent heirs of the silent majority. They are the sons and brothers of middle America. You have the feeling when you come to know them that these men had fathers who had fathers who had fathers who together were the first recruits of this and every other war. It's a rough judgment to make, but it is especially true of the working-class white or black fellow that *but for his desertion* the chances are he would be dead. And somebody else's folks would be asking, "Why?" and saying, "I just can't figure it out."

Helping such people figure it out *now* became a high priority in my own life. I had become—like it or not—an interpreter to middle America of the deserters' situation. The reading I gave of the individual deserter goes something like this:

He comes from a small town or city, often from a rural area; he talks about his "neighborhood" (remember those?)

He's from down home. You'd recognize him, even with a beard.

He has a high school education, on the average.

He's often a second- or third-generation American; his own fore-fathers were immigrants themselves; as often as not they felt conscription or oppression in their time.

He's known a struggle, and he's been around. He has lived marginally most of his life, so he's learned to make do with minimal resources.

He's bought the recruiting sergeant's pitch; career or skill, "join now and go later," "fun, travel and adventure"; later, trained to kill, he feels "sold out."

He waited a year and one-half on the average before he split; he was not quick to take the easy way out.

He's white and comes from a working-class family; or he's black and plain poor.

These Yossarians of America's war in Vietnam are very much alive and well in Sweden, in Canada, in Japan, in Australia, around the globe. They include more than 2,000 in Vietnam. In their profile, they mirror much of the profound crisis of the American experience that deserters from the Korean War called, even then, "the sickness."

Most of us can identify more with the chaplain than with Yossarian in *Catch-22*. Late in the story, Yossarian discovers that his buddy, Orr, has deserted those constant bombing missions and made it to Sweden. And Yossarian says he's going the same route. Sympathetic, the chaplain says, "Wonderful. Run away to Sweden, Yossarian. And I'll stay here and persevere." Most of us, no matter how sympathetic to the message or the plight of the men of this new Exodus, will have to "stay here and persevere." But the American deserters from the American military machine, prosecuting the war in Vietnam, Laos and Cambodia, pose for all of us a question that cuts to the quick. Stay here—for what? Persevere—for whom?

chapter 2

DOING THE RECONCILING THING

I pledge myself to the ministry of reconciliation. To seek
the release of those in prison for conscience' sake, the return in freedom of those in hiding and abroad, and to work
for the rebuilding of America in a world of enduring peace.

—Covenant of the author and the congregation
at the Commissioning of a Ministry in Sweden,
on the steps of the Department of Justice,
Washington, D.C., February 5, 1969

When my wife and I decided to accept our work in that parish
out of bounds in Sweden, we saw ourselves doing the reconciling
thing. Even then we knew our work would be full of tensions
between many groups of human beings, some of whom saw
themselves as enemies of others. We had worked long enough in
the parish ministry, in the city of Pittsburgh and in the antiwar
movement to know that reconciling people to each other and
reconciling ourselves to the things of God is never easy. If it
comes cheaply, it is surely not reconciliation. There is too much
of the enemy in each of us for us to make friends easily or often.
But, as before, we knew this too would be steady work. Serving
in Sweden among the GI's and resisters seemed natural, like
placing one step ahead of another, in the process of working out
our own reconciling thing.

Up the Aisles for Peace

The Sweden Project, as it came to be called, was one of many endeavors of Clergy and Laymen Concerned about Vietnam (CALCAV),* an interfaith organization formed late in 1965 to develop and interpret opposition to the war in American religious communities. I could see from our vantage point in Pittsburgh the great need for just such an organization to surface and focus a prophetic witness. Over the four years of its existence, this organization, along with its older and historically pacifist counterpart, the Fellowship of Reconciliation, had been shaping the spears of *this* war into the hooks of the nation's conscience. CALCAV had extended its campaign into 150 cities and towns; published three books,† supported men of conscience in their draft resistance actions; called three national mobilizations of clergy and laymen; involved people strongly in the Vietnam Summer of 1967; printed more than two and one-half million copies of *"Who's Right? Who's Wrong? on Vietnam,"* a pamphlet used widely in the presidential primaries and local campaigns of 1968; produced with American Documentary Films *Vietnam Dialogue* featuring David Schoenbrun, a former CBS correspondent in Vietnam; and grew to be one of the authentic "bottom up" organizations in the struggle to end U.S. involvement in the Vietnam war.

It was natural, then, that some American delegates to the World Council of Churches meeting in Uppsala, Sweden, in July, 1968, should have evidenced their deep concern for, and sympathy with, the presence of American Vietnam war deserters in Sweden. Several of those delegates arranged for a meeting of Americans with members of the American Deserters Committee

---

* The organization shortened its name in mid-1970 to Clergy and Layman Concerned.

† *Washington and Vietnam,* edited by Dorothy Dunbar Bromley (1966) on the moral and political issues of the war, *In the Name of America,* edited by Seymour Mellman (1968) on war crimes; and *Vietnam: Crisis of Conscience,* by Robert MacAfee Brown, Abraham Heschel, and Michael Novak.

during the World Council deliberations.* On their return, the delegates who were members of CALCAV strongly suggested some kind of initiative to publicize the existence of the deserters and their antiwar motivation. By September a plan was devised by David Dellinger of the (then) National Mobilization Committee to End the War in Vietnam and the Rev. Richard R. Fernandez, Executive Secretary of CALCAV, to have a joint delegation from the two groups go both to Stockholm and to Paris, where a number of American war deserters had also established themselves in exile.

The visit took place in October. "The Delegation," as everyone now refers to it, numbered sixteen persons—clergy, teachers, writers and one mother of a deserter.† Actual contact with the young Americans had a profound affect on the entire team. On their return, several members published articles in newspapers such as the *Christian Science Monitor*, and the *Philadelphia Inquirer* and in magazines such as *Christianity and Crisis* and *Commonweal*.‡ One of the main purposes of the visit had been "to break through the fog of propaganda," as one member put it, and the articles began to do that.

The Delegation was interested especially in the work in Paris where the Rev. William Bloom, an American Presbyterian minister working with the Reformed Church in France, had responsibility for political refugees in Paris and, at that time, for American deserters and resisters as well. Bloom's work served as a

---

* A resolution issued from the Uppsala meeting reflects something of this: ". . . we note a deep sense of concern that uprootedness and homelessness, whether resulting from violence, war and revolution or other causes, such as voluntary exile for reasons of conscience, continues to afflict people in every continent."

† Members of the delegation were: John Cogley, Harvey Cox, Mrs. Marjorie Dunn, David Gracie, Paul Jacobs, Edward Jans, Martin Kenner, Howard Moore, Jr., Richard Neuhaus, Michael Novak, Mrs. Grace Paley, Joseph Sax, Franz Schurmann, Geoffrey Sharlotte, Charles Webster, Jr. and John Wilson.

‡ See *Deserters in Exile,* a collection of these articles. CALCAV, 637 West 125th St., New York, N.Y. 10027 (25 cents).

small-scale model for the possibility of a similar work in Sweden. In fact, most of the work with deserters was being carried on by several Parisians, Americans and other nationals, deeply concerned that the men establish themselves there. The revolutionary days of May, 1968, and the general strike in France posed severe problems for these persons, for the French government had prohibited Americans from political involvement as a condition of their receiving *carte de séjours*, or residence permits. Alleged activity on behalf of the deserters eventually led (October, 1969) to the deportation to Vienna, after a Gestapo-like seizure by French police on the street, of Thomas Schweitzer, an Austrian-born American citizen.

In spite of the French government's prohibition, many of the deserters continued to stay politically active. On May 21, the "French Union of American Deserters and Draft Resisters" held a press conference in the Sorbonne to issue a statement of solidarity with the French students who had taken control of the University of Paris and the French workers who had seized many of their factories. Their statement is indicative of the kind of sentiment found among many, but by no means all, of the deserters and resisters in France and in Sweden.

We Americans who have refused to serve in the U.S. Army in order to resist our country's imperialist wars throughout the third world, have been granted asylum in France on the condition that we swear in writing not to participate in any political activity while we are here. However, we are not simply emigrants from our country. *We are political exiles and we refuse to remain silent.* [Author's italics.]

As an integral part of the American radical movement against capitalist institutions of exploitation and control, we express our complete solidarity with the struggle of French workers and students, in the factories and universities of France.

The French militants, the American radicals, and the third world liberation fronts are, in fact, part of one revolutionary movement. Our enemy is the same: stagnant power structures, fascist repression, capitalist exploitation. We face the same weapons and brutal tactics in Paris, Saigon, and New York.*

Despite the horrifying material power of our enemy, our movement is succeeding. In the spring of 1968 we have seen the student occupation of the University of Paris and Columbia University, successes of the liberation movements in South Vietnam and in the black communities in the U.S. and workers' rebellions in France and Spain, as well as the extraparliamentary student revolts throughout Europe. The brutal repression used by the fascist "services of order" to suppress these movements has served only to increase our determination and resourcefulness.

We join you. . . .

Members of the Delegation also found that a number of the men had opted to live outside Paris in remote rural or town areas. In either case, in or out of Paris, the men were found to be living precariously, with jobs difficult to find and possibilites for mobility limited.

"I am Curious (Red, White and Blue)"

The Delegation found the situation in Sweden more open in terms of the possibilities for jobs and schooling, yet still precarious. One great difference between Sweden and France was important then, and is now. Sweden makes no formal objection to political activity on the part of the Americans there. Our men, like other refugee groups, were free to organize themselves and to express themselves about the nature of their convictions.

Swedish people support the American deserters in their stand and see it as morally honest. The one time some Swedish authorities did try to limit political activity by the Americans, when a "language camp for American refugees" (*Osterbybruk*) was set up in April, 1969, the protest of the deserters and sympathetic Swedes forced the bureaucrats involved to back down.

The problems of the deserter community in Sweden were seen

---

* This is BC—Before Chicago, August, 1968, and the "police riot" during the Democratic National Convention.

to be more generally related to the "duration"—being in exile. One aspect of this sense of a long haul was the uncertainty over just how long the Americans would be permitted to stay. There had been several cases in which deserters or resisters had been ordered to be deported from Sweden, or in which there was a serious hassle with police authorities at Arlanda Airport, Stockholm, or the Gothenburg or Malmoe borders. Such asylum as the men had was not won without a struggle in spite of the Swedish government's protestations to the contrary. Still, in comparison with France, it seemed to the members of the Delegation that most of the problems were related to the business of "making it" in Swedish society, a culture that appears, on the surface, foreign to Americans.

The men in Sweden saw things differently; differently from the Delegation, and differently from one another. For one thing, there was the constant presence of American authorities at the Embassy in Stockholm, and the activity of agents for the Criminal Intelligence Division of the U.S. Army Provost Marshal's Office for Europe, in enticing and persuading men to return to the military. It had not been an idle matter when members of the American Deserters Committee had trapped Mr. William Russell, then with the official newspaper, *Army Times*, in the act of making deals with the men, offering short sentences in the stockades to men who would turn themselves in. The incident has become known as "The Jerum Affair," after the name of the student dormitory, at the University of Stockholm, in which Russell was caught, photographed and taped.

Some men also felt that several members of the Swedish Vietnam Committee had promised support, including political asylum, and then backed down when it was discovered the men had been granted only a "right to stay." Many of the men felt sold out by prominent Swedish supporters on this issue.

Among the deserters themselves there was division, especially on the question of whether the most important goal was "political"—that is, about the question of asylum—or whether it was "humanitarian," centering on the business of jobs, schooling, language and housing. Charges of secret agentry, while common to every exile community, were particularly painful to deal with as they often distracted the men from dealing with issues they all had in common. Paranoid, it is true, many of the men were. But even paranoids have real fears, and there *were* people to watch for and alliances to be careful of. Members of the Delegation found themselves deeply torn by their sympathy for the overall situation of the men, and by the reports they heard from fellows on different sides. Some members, out of either temperament or political judgment, found themselves siding with this or that group among the deserters. Since some of these prominent Americans were associated with Clergy and Laymen Concerned about Vietnam, the deserters themselves drew differing conclusions about the organization, depending on which positions the individual delegates had taken on matters of importance to the deserter community. These judgments, inevitable as they now seem, were to haunt me during my entire ministry in Sweden. Even now, I confess that I do not understand all the dynamics of the visit of the Delegation to Stockholm.

"I think I did the right thing . . ."

On one matter, however, the Delegation was reasonably clear. The men who were in Sweden were political in the sense of their common opposition to the war in Vietnam, even if they were not all political in the more common sense of being committed to a political perspective or organization. John Cogley, of the staff of the Center for the Study of Democratic Institutions, Santa Barbara, California, and former religion editor for *The New York Times,* observed of them:

All are persuaded that the United States has been engaged in monstrous immorality in Vietnam. Many, if not most, have now concluded that the American presence in Southeast Asia, which they regard as murderous, is the inevitable result of a wicked system. The system, they hold, is based on a callous materialism, racism, militarism, social injustice and imperialism. Moreover, they will tell you as quickly as any Columbia or Berkeley activist that the system depends for its life on the blood of the young who have learned to hate the society they are sent into battle to save.*

Mr. Cogley was impressed with the testimony of a twenty-one-year-old white Southerner:

I was a green kid when they drafted me. But I wasn't in the Army long when I began to see that I had been brought up on lies —lies about Negroes, lies about why we were in Vietnam. I looked around in the Army and began to realize that if I had been rich enough to go to college I wouldn't be there. I started to see black men as men and to realize that they weren't treated as equals in the service any more than at home. I started to realize what racism was all about. I got some ideas on my own about the System.

Then I decided that I wasn't ready to die for it and I saw no good reason why I should kill for it. So I made up my mind to split. At first it was just me and the war in Vietnam; desertion is a way of undermining the military power of the U.S.

I think I did the right thing. When America comes to its senses, we'll be thought of as heroes. Hell, we're not alone. Millions of Americans think we have no business in Vietnam. Still most of these same people would say I did the wrong thing in refusing to kill people there.†

This young man was perhaps more articulate than some others but, on balance, he represented the thinking of many of the men as members of the Delegation found them. The Rev. Richard John Neuhaus of the Delegation, and pastor of St. John the Evangelist Lutheran Church, Brooklyn, New York, summed it up this way: "[The deserters] insist they have not deserted America but have, for the sake of America, refused to be agents of its deadly perversion in Vietnam. They want to be part of an America reconstituted in justice, and to be agents of that reconstitution."‡ That is to say, the Delegation found the men politically aware, and by and large politically motivated in their understanding of their actions and the desertion movement.

* Reprinted from *The National Catholic Reporter*, November 13, 1968, by permission of the author.

  † *Ibid.*

  ‡ *The Lutheran Forum,* December, 1968.

The Amnesty Issue: A Matter of Vindication?

Precisely because of this awareness, many of the men in 1968 were interested in the possibility of amnesty. One must remember that in 1968 many Americans believed that there would be a sudden *dénouement* to U.S. involvement in Vietnam as a result of the toppling of the Johnson administration and the election of a new president. Already there were signs that this was an illusion based on hope rather than an analysis of historical proc- ess. But the deserters were caught up in that hope, as were many others. Many asked members of the Delegation about amnesty, and many in the Delegation came with a concern as to what the men in Sweden thought about amnesty themselves.

A little background is necessary here. On August 10, 1968, a group of prominent churchmen, including seven Episcopal and Methodist bishops, pressed for the beginning of a campaign for amnesty for those who were imprisoned or in exile for refusing orders to go into the Army or to fight in Vietnam. Basically, their conviction was that you cannot come to believe that a war is wrong, morally and politically, and then turn your back on the people who have acted out that conviction in their lives. Legal amnesty should follow moral vindication. "Amnesty," the church leaders argued, "would remove the scandal of political imprisonment in America," and would "reflect a nation yet strong and flexible enough to acknowledge its error." Clergy and Laymen Concerned about Vietnam had embarked on a petition- ary campaign to raise the issue of amnesty for the Vietnam war resisters and deserters and by the fall of 1968 had secured thou- sands of signatures. Several senators had indicated their willing- ness to support amnesty on the floor of the Senate when that move became politically viable. So the concern was there.

The Delegation got the impression that many of the ex-GI's wanted to come home if such a possibility were open to them. *At that time*, it is important to underscore. None of the men had then been in Sweden a full year, not even the Intrepid Four. There were perhaps 150 men in all Sweden at that time com- pared with nearly 500 a year and one-half later. They had not as yet been subjected to the long Swedish winters. They had not as yet come to terms with the Nixon administration, with the imminent repression that was to come down on all kinds of dissenting groups from the GI antiwar movement, to the conspiracy trial of the Chicago Eight, to the Black Panther party. Which is to say, they had not come to terms with the "duration" of exile. "We're here for the duration of a rotten time in American life," said Rod Huth, a former Marine.

How Long is a "Duration"?

"For the duration." You never know how long a duration is until it is over. The men in Sweden and in Canada are there for the duration. The longer they are there, the more they must face the prospect of being there permanently. In Sweden, in late 1968, this was just beginning to come into their consciousness. The Delegation, in its enthusiasm for amnesty, unintentionally gave some of the men the impression that it was likely to come to pass regardless of who went into the White House. Nevertheless, the Delegation did come away with the feeling that most of the men were seriously interested in the possibility of amnesty. By the time we arrived in Stockholm in early 1969, just five months after the delegation's visit, we found a rather different set of ideas on the matter. This is one more piece of evidence to show the astonishing growth the men achieved in a time of crisis in their lives. They might be there for the duration, but the situation was changing all the while.

Yet with all the varying impressions and discussions, the sense of internal division in the deserter community and the awareness of problems with the Swedish government, the Delegation was moved profoundly. Dr. Michael Novak, then chairman of the Humanities Department of the State University of New York, Old Westbury, wrote afterward: "Many of us felt humbled; we have written against the war, but we do not face the choice of carrying arms in it or going to jail. We see the political foolishness and moral outrage, but we are not forced into exile. Our conscience is formed easily. These young men carry the cruel burden."* The Delegation called for someone to help carry that cruel burden. The deserters themselves agreed that such a person might be of help, though they later repudiated any implication that they had asked for it.

Clergy and Laymen Concerned moved to find such a person, in the form of a pastor who would spend a year trying to discover what could be done to improve the situation and assist the men in Sweden. The work was set up as a special project—The Sweden Project—to affirm and test the commitment of American churches and synagogues to young Americans who had been deeply alienated by the war and much of the American system that fed the policies of the war. The 1969 position paper of CALCAV, entitled appropriately "The Reconciliation We Seek," noted that "Our time is marked by an ambiguity that defies both contentment and despair." That paper further committed the organization to a continuing work of reconciliation between the American people and American GI's recruited or drafted to fight the war. Especially important was the effort to establish some bridge of communication between the American people and the deserters from military service who were seen as "among the forgotten victims of the Vietnam war." Monies for the project would be raised independently of the ongoing concerns of CALCAV for two reasons: (1) to insure the funding from the beginning and (2) to prevent the implication of some supporters in a project which they or the U.S. government might consider illegal under the federal law, prohibiting, "enticing or procuring" or "aiding or abetting" men "to shrink from hazardous duty."

Flesh and Bones of a Commitment

When my wife and I were asked to take on this ministry, we were then engaged in a meaningful work with the Episcopal Peace Fellowship, a voluntary organization within the Episcopal Church, dedicated to a ministry of reconciliation in the peaceable way of Jesus. One part of our commitment in the Fellowship is to

* *Commonweal*, November 22, 1968.

"wage peace across all boundaries, calling upon men everywhere to repent, to forgive and to love." The Sweden Project seemed like flesh on the bones of that commitment. We saw the ministry among deserters as a duty and as a privilege. We saw it as doing the reconciling thing. Whether we could do it in fact was another matter. But we could not run from it, even though it possibly meant giving up the security of home and job on our return. We simply hoped that we could make available a human presence in the painful ambiguity of exile. We hoped for a new connection between the deserters, their compatriots—the resisters—and the American public.

We framed three goals before we began. We would endeavor:

1. to establish a bridge of communication between the men in Sweden and concerned Americans, especially the parents of these men;

2. to assist in building a relatively stable, relatively independent community of deserters and resisters in Sweden;

3. to work with individuals according to their personal needs as they tried to make it in Swedish society, and to work with the appropriate Swedish authorities.

I remember reading a poem over and over again at the time. It seemed to catch something of the personal risk and adventure in what we were about to do. It is called "Epitaph," and the author is anonymous.*

The subject of the poem was a white postman from Baltimore, Maryland.

> William L. Moore
> Died April 23, 1963
> On U.S. Highway 11 shot in the head with a
>   .22 caliber rifle
> Walking across Alabama with a sign
> EQUAL RIGHTS FOR ALL MISSISSIPPI OR BUST
>
> And a picture of Jesus Christ that agitator
> And a letter to the Governor of Mississippi

* From *Poems of War Resistance*, edited by Scott Bates (New York: Grossman Publishers, Inc. 1969).

"The Mind in Chains" or the
"Autobiography of a Schizophrenic" (1955)

Loco
Loose in the hinges
Jesus
Was a psychopath too
Thought he was the Messiah
He was going to deliver personally

Whether I go forward as Don Quixote
   chasing his windmills or as the pilgrim
   progressing must be left for you to decide

Bill Moore

Pilgrim   Postman

Crucified

We were in no danger of being crucified, but many people thought we were merely chasing windmills, and not progressing. Some of these were in our family and some were our friends. For my part, I felt strangely anointed by our long struggle to end the war in Vietnam to serve in that parish out of bounds.

On February 5, 1969, on the steps of the Department of Justice of the United States, I was "anointed" in fact. Mrs. Martin Luther King, Jr., Rabbi Abraham Heschel, Pastor Richard Neuhaus and Father Richard McSorley did lay their hands upon my head for a "ministry of reconciliation" in Sweden. After the speaking and the singing were over, Mrs. King spoke quietly to me. "Carry it on," she said. "We go with you."

A strange pilgrimage it was to be. Yes, I thought, we were progressing.

chapter 3

WALKING ON WATER

Every raincloud, however fleeting, leaves its mark, not only on trees and flowers whose pulses are quickened, and on the replenished streams and lakes, but also on the rocks are its marks engraved whether we can see them or not.

—John Muir, Founder, Sierra Club

The City of Stockholm floats. People there walk on water, it seems. Called the "Venice of the North," Stockholm includes the northernmost continuously existing Old Town in Europe, Gamla Stan. (In the Old Town there actually is a street named Baggensgatan, reminding one of the character Bilbo Baggins in Tolkien's stories.) During 1969 I practically lived in this old section of the city, where we worked out of an old office building at Malartorget 15, in space loaned to us by the Free Church Council of Sweden.

The City That Became a Parable

I said Stockholm floats. Actually it is built around and on no less than thirteen islands. Arriving in the early spring, you notice this because the ice is jammed up into heavy floes in the center city. You wonder that people survive the long Swedish winter with only that ghostly winter light. There are bridges everywhere; in good weather the ride beneath them is a tourist's dream. You watch the Swedes themselves taking the first look at the sun. In fact, they take a fix on the sun as during their lunch breaks they stand or sit with their faces raised vertically, their bodies frozen as if by the past. You realize immediately that you are watching a ritual. Biorhythm. A kind of social ecology.

It is nevertheless a bit unreal. Perhaps all the associations of a year there have done their duty, but Stockholm seemed then and does now to be floating in an entirely different sense. One well-traveled deserter remarked to me early on that "Stockholm's the most beautiful city in Europe, maybe the world, but it has no 'soul.' " From time to time many of the men would express the same feeling, often by taking off to Helsinki or Copenhagen for some action. Moreover, there was the added contradiction of my coming from New York City, and formerly Pittsburgh, to a city where even the subways are works of art. Östermalm, a kind of Georgetown of Stockholm, has a subway stop on the Tunnelbana to top them all. Like all the stations of the metro, Östermalmstorg has a publicly commissioned work of art; this one was executed by Siri Derkert, an early Swedish feminist and pacifist, now in her seventies. The design has for its theme "peace." The word is seen in a dozen languages, interspersed with the CND-Aldermaston peace symbol, musical bars of the Internationale, slogans denouncing war in general, pesticides and the H-bomb in particular, and the entire mural, sandblasted and sculpted out of the wall, is supported by the great names of Brecht, Sartre, Einstein and Franz Fanon. To my polluted mind it was all too clean to be credible. New York City was never like this, sad to say.

So we began walking on water. The physical impression of Stockholm became for me a parable of the emotional and political experience of working with the deserters. I struggled with them to cross the water from one shore to another. Nothing had quite prepared them for this experience of exile on which they were embarked. Not New York City, not New Hope, Pennsylvania, not any new or old town of their origins. And reading that "litany of origins," the home towns of these fellows, makes one deeply aware of how unlikely it is for them to become transnational in their outlook. Few of these men come from America's great cities, nor are they generally well traveled outside the United States, apart from their military service. I have not the slightest idea what this proves or disproves. It does seem to indicate a deeper wellspring within the American hope than we generally attribute to ourselves. It may only be another illustration of that compulsion of Americans to make of every place a new frontier.

"Like being a Scotch Consultant to Alcoholics Anonymous"

After we were on the job for a while, George, one of the city boys, out of Atlanta, quipped that the whole idea of our Sweden Project of Clergy and Laymen Concerned about Vietnam was "like being a Scotch consultant to members of Alcoholics Anonymous." George had it right in a way. I was not a deserter myself, not even the son of a forefather who had deserted some former European war. I had not even served in the military because of that curious, and I believe class-based, privilege whereby the clergy are automatically exempt from a decision on conscription. (I was not allowed to file for conscientious objector status as a result.) Still, some folks believed I had whatever credentials were necessary out of a rather thorough involvement in the American antiwar movement. I was quickly to discover that another kind of credential was most useful. I am a pastor. My own work permit had it *pastor-kurator*, the latter being a kind of social worker. And these men and women, their wives and girlfriends, were indeed a congregation. The parish was out of bounds, it is true. According to the Uniform Code of Military Justice, these men were not supposed to be there. But there they were. What was anyone to make of it, of them?

The Swedes, we found, were having their troubles on this score. After a great many hassles, a good procedure for entry had been set up. Shortly after a man arrives he must go to the police station, usually the central one in Stockholm at Kungsholmsgatan 35, and file his papers. He must present evidence that he has, in fact, come to Sweden because of his refusal to continue his involvement in the U.S. war on the Vietnamese. That is, he must show either his military identification or his draft status as I-A. The man then applies for political asylum, in spite of the fact that he can never receive this status. He is granted instead, a "right to stay" according to the February 21, 1969, decision of the Swedish government. According to that document:

[American] deserters and other persons who refuse to take part in war activities will as hitherto be granted residence permits in Sweden. Those who run the risk of being sent for service to a theatre of war will be given such asylum. In other cases, the question of asylum will be considered with due regard to the circumstances of each individual case. . . . Deserters and other persons who refuse to take part in war activities have thus the possibility safely to remain in our country. As a result of the special adaptation efforts, conditions are being created for them to adapt themselves and to earn their living here. Against this background it will be of no real importance to them that they, in accordance with a long and firm practice in Sweden, will not be regarded as political refugees when the Aliens' Act is applied only on account of their desertion or their refusal to take part in war activities.*

The "long and firm practice in Sweden" relates to Sweden's own history. Sweden has conscription for national service in the military for a minimum of ten months. In 1901 alone, the year conscription was introduced, Sweden lost 15 per cent of its draft-eligible men. Along with the immense poverty at the time, conscription was one of the motives for the emigration of many Swedes to the United States. Thus, Sweden was not willing to recognize—by granting political asylum—objectors to conscription from another country.

In two important cases, those of Warren Hammerman of Baltimore, a draft refuser, and Michael Day of Saint Louis, a

* Sweden's Minister of the Interior, Mr. Eric Holmquist, explains his country's policy toward the deserters as "not an unfriendly gesture toward the U.S." but an acceptance for "humanitarian reasons." *The New York Times*, October 4, 1969.

twenty-eight-year-old deserter and linguist, orders for deportation had been issued on technicalities of the law. The February ruling of the Interior Minister gave some confidence that the men could be assured of staying permanently. By July, 1969, the new Immigration and Naturalization Board had been set up, and now our men may apply for permanent residence status after two years. After a total of seven years, they may apply for citizenship if they wish. The veteran deserters now have "permanent residence." Some will eventually apply for citizenship, but they will probably be in the minority, for the American deserter in Sweden still sees himself as an American, an American in political exile, in short, a political refugee.

After a period of four to six weeks, a man will hear the result of his application. It is now a matter of course for the application to be approved. With his residence permit, *uppehållstillstånd*, usually at first for six months, comes his work permit, *arbetsstillstånd*. Until the man receives these papers he is under the care, if need be, of the Social Bureau. He may receive $16 to $19 a week and about $50 a month housing allowance during these first weeks. Housing in Stockholm is always a problem for everyone, and the deserters are no exception. One of our most vivid impressions is the husband and wife whom we must have moved five times. When thinking of these human beings one always pictures the bags in hand or the duffelbags over the shoulder. There is a nearly constant internal migration for nine months to a year until, as one fellow put it, "You've drifted around for a while and you find the spot and catch it." There are a lot of misses before you catch it.

When a man gets his papers squared away, he is then under the aegis of the National Labor Market Board. In power this authority is roughly analogous to having the U.S. Department of Labor and the AFL-CIO operating under one roof (which may be the case anyway). The Labor Board acts on behalf of some 35,000 immigrant workers each year. To assure that these people become working members of Swedish society, especially the labor force, the labor authorities run an extensive Swedish language learning program. Operated by various unions and cultural clubs, Swedish classes abound throughout the country. The immigrant attends classes six hours a day, five days a week, for at least two months. He may renew study for another two months, and occasionally for two more months. In return for this program of study the immigrant receives about $160 a month, out of which he must pay all his expenses. Because the standard and cost of living are extremely high, especially in Stockholm, this amount does not stretch very far. It is marginal but it is a real help. And if he doesn't make it to classes he is docked accordingly.

The language class is the first great test a deserter faces as he begins to come to terms with himself, his actions and his new life in exile. Often it is an insurmountable barrier, with fellows only learning the language finally from a Swedish girlfriend. More often, it is both barrier and bridge, in that it forces a man to deal with where he really is and where he is going. I have often been asked to compare the situations of the deserters in Sweden and in Canada, and it seems to me that learning the Swedish language is one *favorable* difference. Once you have gotten that language down, at least enough to converse, you have also crossed over into an acceptance of your political status. The developing awareness is often enough to support the human adventure of living and working and carving out a new frontier for yourself, with drive enough left over to give a little help to your friends. "Boy, you're gonna carry that weight a long time" goes for more than the political responsibility for desertion. It has to cover "exile," as well, or "Man, it'll weight you down." It really will.

The Case of Tom K., ex-M.P.

Tom K. is a good example of the process that begins with desertion and moves to exile and on to permanent emigration. Tom, now twenty-eight, comes from Chicago. He spent one year at Alfred University, then dropped out for three years to work as a pipefitter for the Erie Lackawanna Railroad at Hornell, New York. From there he was drafted. He made it to

E-5 grade after five and one-half years in the Army. He had "re-upped" after two years, before Vietnam "heated up," as he puts it. Assigned to the 287th Military Police detachment in Berlin, this Irish-American (his father had been in the Irish Republican Army and split to the States from his British pursuers) ended up as a noncommissioned officer at "Checkpoint Charlie." In late 1968 a member of his detachment with high security clearance deserted and made it to Sweden. Military intelligence types were upset. Special briefings were held; personal interviews were held with men previously cleared. In one such briefing, Tom advised his two interviewers, when asked what he thought, "They bring down orders for Vietnam on me and I'd split too." They all laughed. Two months later Tom got his orders for Vietnam to the 716th MP detachment at Long Binh jail. Tom had figured to "ride the war out safely," until then. He believed the war to be both immoral and illegal, expecially on constitutional grounds. Tom went through his own checkpoint with his German wife and their one-month-old son late one night. The East Germans were impressed. Tom had no trouble getting across. His only problem was convincing the Germans that he no more wanted their propaganda than he had the Americans' over the Vietnam war. He made it to Sweden on March 5, 1969.

A key factor motivating Tom was his experience with Vietnam veterans through many conversations. They advised Tom of what they had done. Combined with some reading of the material the Army gave him and what he could find elsewhere when he attended a couple of meetings in Berlin as a civilian, he could find no rational basis for the United States' involvement in Vietnam. His experience in Europe, where he observed the American domination of European business and political interests, made him more sympathetic to the charges of United States domination in Southeast Asia.

When Tom arrived, he was held for a while north of Stockholm "until he could be placed." At that time certain Swedish authorities were especially worried by the sizable numbers of American deserters coming into Stockholm. Tom and Chris and little Tommy were sent to a town 100 miles south of Stockholm. In this respect Tom and his family were dealt with in an unusual way, for generally there is no difficulty in choosing where you wish to settle. There are now some 300 men living around Stockholm, fifty in the university town of Uppsala and the remainder scattered about the country. Part of Tom's problem when he first settled was that he was quite isolated. "When I read about or heard about the other Americans here [in Sweden], it seemed like a vague abstraction, and that it was not me that was being referred to." Tom was the only American in a large area, including even the American-related Swedish firms, and did not hear from anyone for three months after his arrival. (Not surprisingly, the American Deserters Committee was then attacking the authorities for trying to isolate men as they had done with Tom.) For a time the K.'s became dependent upon the Swedish government for survival. In fact, one of the depressing things to Tom was the feeling of being trapped and dependent in spite of being healthy and eager to work. A Swedish minister had taken the family rather too much under his wing and smothered them with protection. By the time I discovered Tom, three months after his arrival, he had already begun to separate himself from his benefactors. He also began to get his Swedish down and eventually picked up a job working in a mill of the Holmen paper manufacturers.

Tom's motivation became more rather than less important to him during those early months than at the time of his desertion. "I could never consider myself as being a political type person for all that it implies," he told me. "My lack of education has limited my knowledge of such matters. However, I do not think that it requires an exceptionally bright person to understand what my government wished to do in the bloodbath that it has, and is, carrying out in Vietnam. I also believe that it is an insult to the Americans who are backing that effort. I do not wish to become something that I am not or never could be. I have a quiet anger in these matters and the best thing I have been able to do is to refuse my services to the U.S. Army in this act of aggression."

For a time Tom felt that the language barrier and the cultural barriers would be too much for him. He considered going to Canada to remain there permanently. On the possibility of being amnestied, he said, "We have considered the possibility but we have concluded that even if this were to occur it may be just the start of our problems and not, as some believe, the end." Several months later, six months after his arrival, I met with Tom and his wife again. He had given up all thought of going to Canada, which he came to see as "just running away." No longer dependent in any way on the Social Bureau for aid, he was able to support his wife and child on his pay from the mill. Eighteen months have passed since then. Still he works hard and long shifts, but he is happy in doing what he has to do, a remarkable feeling for anyone. He is determined to make it in the town where they were resettled and has assisted several other deserters in settling there too with jobs as well.

One fellow was quite young, barely nineteen, and had found the going in Sweden difficult. I arranged for him to move to Tom's city where Tom could keep an eye on him. Tom was especially sensitive and wisely tough with him. We had worried over this young fellow and feared that he would end up in trouble with the police. Tom remarked about that from the Army side. "Sure, some fellows got in trouble in the Army, but what is an offense to the military is never an offense in civilian life. I know. I was an MP. And most of these guys had only AWOL charges or simply were off base without a pass. I don't call that trouble-making. Trouble is what the Army makes." Tom wanted less trouble and more chances for his young American compatriot.

Tom's feelings run deep. "How I see the U.S. since I have been out of it for over two years—I see its power. I can feel its power despite the fact that I am 6,000 miles away. There's never been anything like it, true. But look what it does with its power. People will soon forget this war as they have all our others. Every 4th of July the politicians will expound upon the glorious battles of Vietnam. The VFW will march and before long our children's textbooks will give a completely different picture than what occurred. I wonder if it will be said in history [books] that a good many Americans opposed this war. I somehow doubt it. After all, have we not found ways to justify the Spanish-American war or our own war with Mexico in 1848? Have we not been able to satisfy ourselves upon our constant interference in the affairs of any country smaller than our own?"

He reflected a lot on meeting me, it turned out. "When I became aware that you had come to Sweden, and that you were a minister, I thought you might have come to sell us a little religion. However, after meeting you, I am convinced that you have come for more earthly reasons. I hope you know what it means to give us some advice on direction toward the future, so that we do not stop our lives here in Sweden because we do not wish to follow in the footsteps of the establishment. This is not to imply that I do not consider myself to be a Christian. Although that is about as far as it goes. I rather like the thought of a life hereafter, particularly since the one I have could stand some improvement. But I'm not in a very big hurry to see it.

"I had a position of some responsibility; I was NCO. When I left Berlin I had little or no plan. Because of this we have lost everything we had, including our clothes, which I have not been able to replace as yet. For this reason I feel that I must make my future plans more carefully so as not to repeat this mistake. I hope you understand the way I feel," he added. "I have never been in any trouble nor do I have a criminal record of any kind any place. The only thing I have ever done has been desert the Army and I do not consider it a crime. I consider it my duty!"

I heard from Tom in a letter recently. He is still at the mill, still settling in, still helping out his friends. He and Chris will stay in Sweden. He says there is lots of overtime at the mill and that he "likes to be first in line." Then he calls out again for help. Through me, I guess, to the reader, to all the people of this land. "I hope you can help some of these people here by making the American people understand what this is all about. Not so much for myself. I can make out, but some of these people cannot. They need help. Don't forget them. Too many of the Americans who influenced them are now forgetting them."

Tom is probably right. Few people realize how profoundly their own doubt about the war policies has inspired the resistance to the war inside the Army. Anyone who ever marched or pamphleteered or even questioned his or her government's Vietnam policies surely has a duty to remember he is, de facto, an aider and abettor of the massive revolt against this war inside the Army.

Assist from the Pentagon

What we found early on in Sweden, though, was that it is the Pentagon and successive American administrations waging war in Vietnam that are the chief aiders and abettors of the GI's resistance to and desertion from this war. Nothing made this more clear than the case of Edwin Arnett, an Army man who had deserted during a five-day leave in Japan and come to Sweden via the Soviet Union. Arnett turned himself in early in 1969. At the time Arnett was on trial at Fort Dix, New Jersey, the Senate Armed Services Sub-Committee on the Treatment of Military Deserters, headed by Senator Daniel Inouye of Hawaii, was meeting in Washington. The Defense Department chose that occasion to release for the first time current figures on the rate of desertion from the U.S. armed forces.

According to this early 1969 report of the Defense Department, the number of deserters from U.S. military forces in fiscal 1967 was 40,277. In fiscal 1968 (to June 30) this number had risen to 53,357. In addition, there were 135,000 AWOL in 1967 and 155,000 in 1968. (A soldier who is absent for more than thirty days is classified as a "deserter"; gone less than thirty days, he is merely "absent without leave.") This amounted to more than 500 AWOL's a day, or one man going over the hill temporarily every three minutes and one going over the hill to stay every ten minutes. (By late 1969 the Pentagon estimated more than 73,000 deserters for 1969 and 225,000 men going AWOL.) The more the orders for Vietnam came down, the tougher the resistance to them became. The report called for more prosecutions of the "military absentees," as they are euphemistically called, and stiffer punishments all around. The soldiers were getting off lighter than their civilian brothers in the resistance, it was charged. Specialist-4 Edwin "Pappy" Arnett, an Army cook in Camranh Bay, of Santa Ana, California and a sometime resident of Sweden, was sentenced to four years at hard labor and given a dishonorable discharge the *same* day, March 6, 1969, that the Inouye Committee came in with its report.

To the men in Sweden the message was clear. No more playing games with the Embassy. No more deals with "the Man." The Arnett case closed the door to the general mass of deserters for "turning yourself in." Arnett's case was all the more poignant to Swedes and Americans alike, who all knew he was mentally sick. I remember talking with Mrs. Svedin, a Swedish social worker who knew Mr. Arnett. She told me, "When I heard about him I couldn't sleep for four nights it disturbed me so. Four years in prison! In prison! That man was so sick he belongs in a hospital. How can they not see that? I am made sick by your sickness in America."

In any case, what we found in those days was a decided turn toward hope among the men in Sweden. For the first time it seemed that some of them realized "once there was a way to get back home," but now, well, "you can't go home again." Even four months earlier, during the visit of the American Delegation from CALCAV and "the Mobe" in October, 1968, one great concern of the men had been about the possibilities for a general amnesty. Now this was out. Any talk about amnesty was considered politically immature. The colors of Nixon and Agnew and Mitchell and Laird, those Four Horsemen rehearsing for the Apocalypse, were already becoming clear. The Chicago indictment was in (the prosecution of the Chicago Eight was announced in late March, 1969). Sweden seemed to be "where it was at"—Sweden, Canada and France. Previously, light sentences had been used to induce the deserters to return.

Donald P. Williams of Chicago and Jackson, Mississippi, a black fellow who was for a time co-chairman of the American Deserters Committee, said he had returned "to do my time and then work with my people." Williams got a six-month sentence but no discharge. The guys questioned whether there was any use in returning if you could not even break out of the Army on the deal. Clearly the Pentagon had moved to change its policy. Repression was to be the final solution for the GI "trouble-makers" and "misfits." If there had been an official declaration of war on Vietnam, no doubt some poor fellow would have been shot as "an example," like Private Eddie Slovik, executed for desertion in World War II, the only American to be so "punished" since the Civil War.*

"Making It" as Fighting Back

In this war and this time it worked the other way. It began to dawn upon many of the most politically aware deserters, and on others who did not see themselves politically involved, that a sure way to block the power of the system was "to put it all together" in Sweden. Here the men were faced with charges that they were traitors, that they were misfits, that they were drop-outs, in effect, that they would never make good any-where. Prove the brass wrong! Prove our position right by mak-ing it here, they reasoned. Take your "R and R" in Sweden and make it stick. Men were coming in every day and when the weather broke sometimes three or four men would arrive in a

---

* See The Execution of Private Slovik, by William Bradford Huie (Little, Brown, 1954). In March, 1970, an anonymous obituary for Eddie Slovik appeared in Stockholm's morning daily newspaper, Dagens Nyheter, on the twenty-fifth anniversary of his execution. The next day a story followed. The obituary remained anonymously placed, but a re-porter told the story. Slovik was quoted as he had told the sergeant who prepared him for the actual shooting: "I'm okay. They're not shooting me for deserting the United States Army. Thousands of guys have done that. They just need to make an example out of somebody and I'm it because I'm an ex-con. I used to steal things when I was a kid, and that's what they are shooting me for. They're shooting me for bread and chewing gum I stole when I was twelve years old."

day. Thus it became expedient, and humanly necessary, to run down every lead on a job, to fight for housing and to learn their way around the Swedish bureaucracies. "Rap" sessions were held on how to do your police interview, how to start out in the language, where to get extra help if you needed it, how *not* to alienate your social bureau and so on. It was transparent to me that all this was enormously political, that you could not separate the humanitarian kinds of help that we could give from the development of community consciousness on the part of the men. When a man first comes, for example, one of his great problems is *who* he is *outside* "The Green Machine." Finding out involves not only coming to accept his act of desertion but also that inner journey of Everyman on the road to discovering himself. Recognizing your own class background, what the military has done to you, who you are and what you were about had to be set in the context of a new way of living. In such circumstances, just finding a pad for a man to start him out can be as political as putting out an entire newsletter, especially when a man has just come in from the no-man's-land of the European underground.

Happily, many of these young Americans have begun to make it in Swedish society. It is a marginal existence, close to the edge of poverty, but most of the men have lived on that edge all their lives. By and large they are from working-class backgrounds, black and white; some have been truly poor all their lives. Never once did I meet one who came from an affluent home. Those who are middle-class have never had it so good that they cannot remember the struggle their parents had in bringing them up. They are highly unlikely candidates for what they did, and yet here they are, making it. Their sense of dignity has increased and their confidence in their actions has deepened. In the year I spent in Sweden I never met a man who regretted his act of desertion. Many a fellow has spent hours reflecting on it; some have returned. Even then, they have decided to take another step for personal, sometimes political, reasons. They have stopped looking over their shoulders at "the Man" and begun moving out.

A Good Report Card

In November, 1969, an interesting report was released by the *Invandraverket*, the Immigrants and Naturalization Board, which supports this judgment. In April, 1969, a remarkable young Swedish social worker, Mrs. Kristina Nystrom, began work among the Americans on behalf of the Swedish government. She has managed to gain the trust of the men regardless of their differences and backgrounds. Mrs. Nystrom reported that she had contact with 294 deserters (out of 378 who had been in contact with the Swedish authorities and 325 who had been granted residence). One hundred and four were working, 103 were in Swedish language classes, seven were in folk high schools, nine were in adult *gymnasia*, six were in training schools, twenty-six were in universities, and fourteen were in the refugee language school–camp in Osterbybruk. Thus more than 90 per cent of the men had put something together, a far cry from the reports of the Pentagon's public relations department and the American Embassy in Stockholm. Mrs. Nystrom found that the "criminality rate among these boys is very low." (A syndicated story by Don Cook of the *Los Angeles Times,* October 12, 1969, alleged that one out of six men had been in trouble in Sweden and that this "constitutes one of the highest crime rates for a relatively small number of men anywhere in the world.") According to Swedish figures, 22 men had served or were serving some time in prison. The Director of the *Invandraverket*, Mr. Kjell Oberg, remarked that "our purpose is to do whatever we can to help these boys become psychologically and physically strong persons." On another occasion, Mr. Oberg told me, "Suppose some day these men should return. It is not in our interest to send psychological wrecks [home] when we can help them here." Mr. Oberg remembered that things had turned around. Once it was America's turn to take Sweden's refugees; now it was about face. He smiled ironically.

There is a well-known writer in Sweden, Vilhelm Moberg, whose story, *The Immigrants*, is being made into film starring Max von Sydow. Moberg has written an epic work on the Swedish immigrants to the United States. In a more recent book, *The Unknown Family*, he wrote:

The United States is no longer that country to which rebels and revolutionaries flee. Just this category of people are instead now leaving the U.S.A. and are going in exile to Canada and Europe. For me these Americans fulfill the great heritage of freedom of their country, in reality they are faithful to this heritage. These are Americans who will not fail that proud proclamation in the Declaration of Independence from July 4, 1776.

Thousands have gone into exile rather than be part of this nation's immoral and illegal involvement in Southeast Asia and the concomitant repression at home. The American people are being sold the pig of world domination in the poke of domestic repression. A lot of Americans aren't buying that any more as being "faithful to this heritage." An estimated 80,000 draft resisters and military deserters are now in Canada. More than 2,000 deserters roam Europe, and many settle in Sweden. Thousands are underground in their own country, exiles at home. And the Exodus continues through the desert of totally discredited death-dealing policies. In this time of crisis I found some of these young Americans in Sweden. They are standing very tall. For a while it seems they are walking on water. It seemed that way to me. But then just beyond you could see beneath the surface that ground was rising up to meet them. They are finding that ground, common to the hope of America, and holding it.

By their mere existence, these men *are* their message. Call them America's first troop withdrawals from Vietnam—Tom and Vince and Buz and Terry and Richard and thousands more. How can we who now find our militarism in Vietnam and violence at home unconscionable turn our backs on those who have acted of similar convictions? If it should not be these sons and brothers, then whose sons, whose brothers?

One humorous incident says it all. Late in the summer Mike came to me to complain about a buddy who had hit him for a loan of 50 crowns ($10) and then had not paid him back. I said, "Come on, Mike, you know you're in the same boat. Give him a break. He'll come around." I wasn't so sure of that but Mike reflected for a moment and then said, "Yeah, that's right, if he's a deserter he can't be all bad, can he?"

chapter 4

"DON'T MOURN. ORGANIZE!"

While there is a lower class, I am in it!
While there is a criminal class, I am of it!
While there is a soul in prison, I am not free!

Love is the greatest power in the Universe.
You must learn to love!

—Eugene Victor Debs

Carrying the weight of their actions while trying to walk on water is hard work, as the deserters and resisters were learning. Learning. It is not something they knew in advance, and needed only to apply. Just as there is little in American experience to prepare us for anything like the condition of exile, there is little in our educational institutions that teaches us how to organize a common life and to practice the application of something that approaches love. On the contrary, much of the learning experience of us all in this society—and the men and women in exile are no exception—is so negative in regard to the possibility of genuine democracy that we must unlearn many things while we track down the few things necessary to that common life.

Strange as it may seem, when it comes to survival patterns, being an American is a handicap. For all the myth-story about our "frontier mentality" as Americans, the actual practice of taking control over and responsibility for our lives is as rare these days as genuinely new frontiers. You have to dig deep to

55

find the springs of hope when simple optimism is no longer pumped in or when the city's reservoir has run dry.

One thing you learn in such circumstances, in a hurry, is to get over the big hang-up of dependency that has characterized your past experience. Your motto has to be those words of Joe Hill, one of America's great labor organizers in the era before World War I, "Don't mourn [for me] . . . Organize!"

Joe Hill, the "Wobbly" (IWW, Industrial Workers of the World) was executed in Salt Lake City in 1915, in spite of pleas by the president of the United States, the government of Sweden and the American Federation of Labor. In 1914 Hill had led an important strike in that city. In a case many historians consider a frame-up, he was later accused and convicted of killing a former policeman who had become a local grocer. Hill's legacy has been personalized in the slogan of the last words heard from him as he died.

Not many Americans know that Joe Hill was a Swede, born in Gävle, a city on Sweden's east coast, and an immigrant to the United States as a young man. Bo Widerberg, director of the film, *Elvira Madigan*, has done a movie about Hill, and a new generation of Americans can rediscover him. It is hard for me to think of Joe Hill without thinking how apt the slogan associated with him is to the work of the American Deserters Committee in Stockholm, in Paris, in Montreal, in Toronto, in Vancouver. Indeed, it is true for all attempts at organizing in exile. When much of the world was pitying these men, they refused to pity themselves and began to get it together—to organize.

Getting It Together

Organizing among the young Americans leaving the U.S. armed forces did not begin immediately as their numbers increased strikingly in 1967. There was a lag of some six to nine months before they found public association necessary to their situation. This corresponds closely to the pattern that developed around active-duty GI organizing done in the States. The work among GI's through the coffee house movement, originally inspired by Fred Gardner, was greatly encouraged by Summer of Support activities in the Vietnam Summer of 1967. At the same time, Andy Stapp and others had organized the American Serviceman's Union, beginning at Fort Sill, Oklahoma.* All these efforts at group association among GI's were preceded and sustained by many acts of individuals at considerable cost to themselves.

In Europe the American Deserters Committee had its beginning in the winter of 1967–68 when more men were, quite literally, taking "French leave" in Paris.† With the announcement by the Swedish government of its acceptance of the Intrepid Four, men began to arrive steadily in that country as well. Through a network of German, Belgian and Dutch underground contacts, men were being passed from their bases in Germany to some measure of safety. At the same time a much smaller number were getting out of Vietnam via Japan and the Soviet Union, euphemistically called by some "the high road." By March, 1968, it was clear that a sizable community of political refugees from American militarism was going to be in Sweden for some time.

For a while incoming men received a number noting the order of their arrival. There are many men still in Sweden who remember themselves as "Number 10," "Number 34" and so on. There were certainly enough men for an organization, and there was plenty of work to be done. For their own lives as deserters (and later, when they were included, for the resisters) the men had a responsibility: to gain a sense of identity, to get processed, to get housing, to find jobs, to learn the language.

* Fred Gardner has written an excellent study of the case of the Presidio 27, *The Unlawful Concert* (Viking Press, 1970). Andy Stapp's book, *Up Against the Brass* (Simon and Schuster, 1970), tells the remarkable story of the A.S.U.

† The phrase "taking French leave" originated with the practice in eighteenth century France of going away from a reception without excusing oneself to the host or hostess. I am told that the French call the same behavior, *s'en aller a l'Anglais*, which must show that desertion is a more universal act than the colonels think.

From the beginning, however, a working distinction was made between this effort and a second, more public one: interpretation of their actions and their situation to the Swedish public, and by way of the American press, to the American people. Much of the early work centered around the priority given to organizing their base of support among the Swedish people. Their political activity, as they saw it, consisted of solidifying their presence in Sweden so that many more GI's could come *and stay*, and in turn get their antiwar message out to Americans at home.

A press conference was called for March 15, 1968, to announce the formation of the ADC and to attack the CID (Criminal Intelligence Division, U.S. Army) for its involvement in the case of Roy Ray Jones, who had been persuaded to return to his unit. Statements were made at that time by co-chairmen Bill Jones, a former medic based in Pirmasens, Germany, at the Second Field Hospital, and Don P. Williams, a regular Army soldier. The word was going out from Stockholm and from Paris, from all over: GI's who were fed up with the war, with army life, did not have to hide or go it alone. There was an organization, the American Deserters Committee, committed to their welfare and in touch with groups throughout Europe ready to help find a new home, a new job, a fresh start in political exile. Calling cards were passed out on bases saying, "BE A MAN, NOT A WAR MACHINE. DESERT."

Thus, from the beginning the men's identity as military deserters was "up front," a point that cannot be stressed too strongly. For centuries, the word "deserter" had been synonymous with treason, or cowardice under fire. Now it was being turned against the same military establishment that used such language to separate, isolate and imprison its victims. The simple fact, clear enough from all the records and verified in my own experience, is that these men were and are genuinely proud of having deserted the armed forces of the United States of America.

"Refuse at all costs . . . this madness"

In the beginning the full title of the organization was The International Union of American Deserters and Draft Resisters. This reflected a concern for those in France who were, in fact, draft resisters—having refused or avoided induction—rather than GI's who had left. In *The Second Front*, a bulletin published at first from Paris, one of the prime reasons for organizing was said to be the necessity of self-defense and protection. "We feel it is important," Issue One read, "to discuss organizing at this time both to increase our number and to maintain the support of friends necessary to provide for our continued security in exile. U.S. authorities would have a much more difficult time bothering anyone who had the strength of numbers and popular opinion behind them."

This statement anticipated a practice that was to become important in Sweden: the activity there of plain-clothed representatives of the CID from the Army Provost Marshal's office in Heidelberg, Germany. The little bulletin concluded its statement of purpose with a look toward the "mother country." "It is only by organizing that we can remove the causes for desertion and draft refusal, and finally only by organizing that we can return to our country as free men." The editors added, however, that "returning is clearly a choice for each individual."

On April 3, 1968, the American Deserters Committee of Sweden called its second press conference and made the following statement to the people of the United States. It is a political message by the deserter community, and is instructive not only for what it says but also for the insight it gives into the image the men had of themselves. Before the assassinations of Martin Luther King, Jr. and Robert Kennedy. Before Chicago.

With each new day dissent against the war in Vietnam grows. Demonstrations and protest marches occur in Washington, New York, Paris, and throughout the world. Eminent doctors, philosophers, and scientists voice their dissent in public speeches. And still the escalation continues. Every month the draft quota grows, more and more troops are sent to fight and die in the most brutally oppressive war of our times. Protest seems to bounce harmlessly off the walls of the Pentagon. Our country's leaders, impervious to all arguments and blind to all show of dissent, continue unhindered in their insane policy of decimating the Vietnamese people in the name of liberty and freedom. Our president has called for a stop to the bombing. Thank God for that. [Author's note: The next day, April 4, the Vietnamese agreed quickly to come to Paris for a peace conference.] But this is no solution. He has asked for negotiations. But what indeed can the Vietnamese people negotiate? There is one solution and only one—that the U.S. withdraw immediately and unequivocally from Vietnam.

And as our concern is focused on this war, the domestic situation gets worse. The black ghetto is used as a recruiting center for needs in Vietnam. This policy has a two-fold purpose: (1) to act as a deterrent for further racial violence, (2) to fill in the gaps left by those fallen in Vietnam, the majority of whom had also been Afro-Americans. The two struggles, the black man's struggle for freedom and the struggle to end the war in Vietnam, are both part of a bigger struggle, the struggle against the insane and inhuman policies of U.S. imperialism.

The only way to stop this war seems to be for everyone who can be used in its continuation to *refuse at all costs to contribute themselves to this madness.* (Author's italics) Workers in the arms industries must refuse to work; dock workers must refuse to load ships bound for Vietnam; scientists employed in finding new and more effective methods of destruction must refuse to continue research; young men due to be drafted must refuse to go; and soldiers in the U.S. Army must refuse to contribute to that arm of destruction.

We, ex-soldiers, who have come to Sweden, have done just that. We have refused to participate in any way with an organization which carries on all the death and destruction in Vietnam. We choose to live in exile rather than to be used as pawns in the deadly game of world imperialism. We found that our duty to the rest of mankind and to the Vietnamese people far outweighed our duty to the U.S. Army. A choice of loyalties had to be made. We chose to be loyal to our fellow men and therefore to ourselves.

And each day more men come to Sweden, motivated by the same loyalty, and for each man that comes, there is one less man that can be used for the futile aggression in Vietnam.

We, the deserters and draft resisters in Sweden, unite ourselves in an International Union with all the groups of deserters and draft resisters in France, Holland, England and all the other countries that are harboring deserters and draft resisters. We appeal to the people of the United States who realize the uselessness of this war and the blindness of the U.S. foreign policy, to support us in our actions. We still need assistance in our efforts to take care of each man who comes to Sweden and we will need support to make changes within the U.S. in order to create favorable conditions for our eventual return there.

We express our unity with the people in the United States and the rest of the world who are actively working to oppose this war. As our numbers swell and as our unity grows stronger with other groups working for the same goals, we will eventually be able to bring the despicable war machine of the U.S. to a standstill, which will in turn clear the air for a greater possibility of peace and freedom throughout the world.

This statement became a charter of purpose for many a new man searching for his human identity, for confirmation of his antiwar and anti-imperialist motivation and for a new life. From the beginning these young men spoke as Americans to other Americans. While they question what has happened to America and to themselves as Americans, they do not question their Americanism. They assume their involvement in a common struggle to end the oppression monstrously illustrated to them by America's war in Southeast Asia.

Yet so constant has been the effort by the American military and established press to picture these persons as "stateless,"*

* A particularly sad example of this kind of journalism is found in articles by Bruce Bahrenburg, of the *Newark* (N.J.) *Evening News*, April 13–18, 1969. One article was entitled: "Men Without a Country."

The United Nations Convention relating to the Status of Stateless Persons defines such a person as one "who is not considered as a national by any State under the operation of its law." As the Uniform Code of Military Justice of the U.S. armed forces is still considered binding if not un-American, it is necessary to underline their own conviction that they too are part of the struggle. With millions of their fellow-Americans they too wanted to "clog with their whole weight" to bring the war machinery to a halt.

"Agit-prop"

In those days, from early 1968 through early 1969, the primary spokesman for the ADC was William "Bill" Jones, of St. Louis, Missouri. In the Army for over a year, and trained as a combat medic, Jones was assigned to Vietnam from Germany. At that point, his long-standing opposition to U.S. involvement in the affairs of other nations pushed him to a personal edge. He deserted to Sweden. Later many others from his unit were to follow him. Bill Jones is lean and tall, rather precisely handsome in appearance, and given to considerable intellectual prowess. Were Bill a convinced capitalist, he might be a spokesman for the Junior Chamber of Commerce.

A former Roman Catholic seminarian, he brought to the exile community a sensitivity to a people-oriented rhetoric that was immediately appropriated by his brothers in struggle. For many months he took the lead in publishing articles for *The Second Front* (for GI's), in arranging with a delegation of the Democratic Republic of Vietnam for "Radio Second Front" broadcasts to U.S. troops in Vietnam and in relations with the press. His personal abilities so dominated much of the efforts of the ADC that he later became an issue himself. To his credit, Bill has been able to take more of a back seat by giving over more and more responsibility to others.

The efforts of the ADC were directed, of course, not only toward the people back home but toward the GI's themselves. For "agit-prop"—agitation and propaganda—it would be very

---

upon military personnel who have removed themselves from active jurisdiction of military bases, American deserters are not stateless persons. Further, they may not lose their citizenship in any manner other than to voluntarily give it up.

hard to find anything more effective with line GI's than the following "rap" by Jones:

> They call you a man, and treat you like an animal;
> They feed you their line, and you think it's the truth.
> Remember in basic training: double time, chow line, right face, left face.
> They wanted you disciplined like a well-running machine, easy to control, easy to handle. They gave you a trade, and called you a soldier.
> A soldier: a man ready to die for a cause they call your own, to kill a man they call your enemy.
> And you believed it; you swallowed the story lock, stock, and barrel.
> And after being so generous, and making you a man, and making you a soldier, they're ready to do you more favors.
> They clothe you, and feed you, and pay for your transportation to the war, or wherever they need you.
> And when you die, they'll pay for your funeral.
>
> Uncle Sam needs you—to stop the bullets, to smother the grenades, to make the world safe for Coca-Cola.
> Where will Uncle Sam go next—to Thailand, Cambodia, Bolivia or Guatemala (there are already Green Berets there), Santo Domingo (they've tried that before)?
> There seems to be no end in sight.
>
> They made you a man, did they? Well, now show them how a man really acts. A man makes his own decisions, and if you decide that you can't go along with Uncle Sam and his endless, constant wars, then you can leave.
> It can be done, and many have already done it.
> You can come to Sweden; there are many people and organizations ready to help you.
>
> What's required of you is a man's decision.
> Stop letting Uncle Sam make your decisions for you!

Agents at Work?

But the situation was not all that smooth in Sweden, even in the beginning. As I was to learn from even my brief encounters with the Greek refugee community in Sweden, most exiles deal sooner than later with the presence of agents. For one who has not experienced the real possibility of being hijacked on the streets, or being documented by an informer, it is hard to imagine how real indeed is that threat. An exile community needs only one or two incidents to make it wary of strangers: unusual telephone calls, sudden visitors, even new additions to the exile community. And, as W. I. Thomas put it, "If men define situations as real, they are real in their consequences."

Quite real in its consequence for the deserters was the "Jerum Affair", so named because it took place in the Jerum dormitory of the University of Stockholm. William Russell, an American civilian editor of a military newspaper had been involved, in the spring of 1968, in the arrangement made by agents of the CID with Roy Ray Jones for his return to his unit in Germany. That "deal" was apparently considered a success by the military authorities because Russell returned, according to his unwitting admission, with orders to secure the return of several more deserters. A trap was set for Mr. Russell by members of the American Deserters Committee in a dormitory room of the University of Stockholm. From the deserters' point of view Mr. Russell was indeed an agent.

Mr. Russell's own intentions may have been otherwise. Clearly, on the evidence of tapes and photographs of the scene, and the fact that he was involved in Jones' return, his efforts were authorized by the U.S. military forces.

A further consequence of the exposé was that several officials of the American Embassy, implicated in the affair, were sent home from Sweden. Whether or not this resulted from the publicity surrounding the affair is unknown. Not a few Americans and Swedes believe that the ensuing embarrassment to the American ambassador, William W. Heath, was more a factor in his eventual return to Washington than the (then) impending change in U.S. administrations.

Will "Shakespeare" V., an Army deserter from upstate New York, had his own solution to the interventions by the American Embassy in Stockholm. "Shakespeare" is one of the few natural humorists in the community. He proposed that the ADC get up a petition to Merle Arp, Deputy Chief of Mission, and suggest that the Embassy split the costs of the mounting ADC office telephone bills down the middle. That way, said Will, ADC saves money and the Embassy saves the price of at least one agent. ADC telephones were assumed to be tapped. "See how we love our country," he added. "We even save the taxpayers' money."

The Jerum Affair was an enormous victory for the ADC. Externally, it showed the people of Sweden that agents of the U.S. military complex were not figments of the young exile imagination. Internally, it proved to the deserters and resisters themselves the absolute necessity of organizing for survival. Bill Jones, Don Williams and all the others who had hung together in the first flush of rhetoric and adventure were vindicated. Young Americans who felt sold out by being recruited for careers and then trained only for war saw themselves pursued still, even into exile. Their backs were stiffened by experiencing continued oppression.

The effect in the Swedish press and on public opinion generally was startling. To interpret their presence in Sweden, the ADC moved on to publish (in Swedish) a well-edited and produced magazine entitled *The Second Front Review*. Work began on *Deserter, U.S.A.*, a movie directed by two young Swedish directors, Olle Sjogren and Lars Lambert. A new problem—the contradictions within Swedish policy—began to surface, and the men tried to deal with it. What the men saw in Swedish policy was a strange ambivalence that was potentially dangerous to them. On the one hand, Sweden was making a great deal of political hay out of its policy of asylum, at least in some international circles. At the same time, middle-level

Swedish bureaucrats took an extraordinarily long time in processing applications for asylum, gave many different reasons to many different men for the granting or denial of social help and generally seemed quite uncertain that the deserters were welcome at all.

A Reality Trip

The effect of this struggle toward interpretation coupled with the given-ness of trying to make a new life was, as some of the romance wore off, a "reality trip." Soon after the Jerum Affair there began to develop a kind of split or fault among the deserters themselves. Well before any organizational division, there came to be something like the dissociation that frequently takes place within an individual under great stress. The increasing pressure of the politically volatile and humanly fearsome situation—the *reality* of the world as compared with its appearance —began to be so threatening as to force a retreat into their internal struggle for some kind of personal and corporate identity. Dominating discussions in the group was increasingly the question of *who* was making decisions rather than what those decisions were to be. The human error of backbiting and gossip was not without its toll, as well. In retrospect, many men see that they were "growing up" the hard way. (But is there any other way?)

The film, *Deserter U.S.A.*, for example, so depicted the men as heroes, and yet so parodied the Swedes, that finally it was not credible even to those who had acted in it. Filmed in late summer, 1968, it was shown in the early spring, 1969. During that time span, a winter has passed, and the men had been both toughened and made wiser by the work of the intervening months. The incidents on which the movie was based actually occurred, and the Swedish citizens involved were shown as they were perceived at the time—as often as not, tools of the United States. But in nine months the men had become a little less sure of themselves, and less eager to "expose" the Swedes, so that a good deal of effort was spent in using the film to interpret their progress to and through Swedish support groups throughout the country. In my opinion, it took the three short personal statements appended to the film at its end—statements spoken in Swedish—to save the movie and, by inference, give some validity to the material that formed the body of the story. The failure of the film to become a first-rate document of the Swedish scene, which could have been quite useful in the States, stems, I think, from the dissociation process taking place at the time. Reality had outrun their fantasies, and the men had not figured that out.

By the time the Delegation representing Clergy and Laymen Concerned about Vietnam and the National Mobilization Committee to End the War (later known as the "New Mobe"), arrived in the fall of 1968, two things were becoming clear. First, the issue of political asylum had become preeminent for the ADC when one resister and one deserter were threatened with expulsion from Sweden on legal technicalities. Second, an increasing number of men were becoming dissatisfied with the organization of the ADC. The situation was so confusing to the visitors that, as they talked to one man and then another, they could not tell whom to believe. In turn, various members of the deserter-resister community saw different members of the Delegation as friends or as foes. In the intense atmosphere of that first formal meeting between representatives of the movement—at home and in exile—it was virtually impossible for people to be heard as individuals.

Political asylum became the primary organizing focus of the American Deserters Committee in Sweden when it was discovered in struggle that they did not have it. Until the cases of Warren Hammerman, of Baltimore, Maryland, and Michael-Henri Day, of St. Louis, Missouri, it was generally believed by the men that they *had* the certainty of asylum. With the threat of deportation coming down upon two of the men, suddenly no one was safe. What happened between prominent members of the Swedish Vietnam Committee, most of whom are members of the ruling Social Democratic party, and the deserters, to create this enormous misunderstanding is still not clear to me.

And I have talked about it with our men who were involved, men with opposite interpretations, and with representatives of the Swedish government and the Swedish Vietnam Committee, including that group's chairman, Bertil Svanstrom.* Whatever actually transpired, the men came to believe that they were at best misled, and at worst deceived, by the Swedish Vietnam Committee and the Swedish government. Fuel was added to the fire when it was rumored in the Swedish press that the National Labor Market Board, combining labor and government interests, was thinking of a quota beyond which no more American war resisters would be welcome. (I discovered much later from a Swedish official that this rumor had substance at the time, but that the proposal was opposed and defeated within the government.)

Certain members of the Swedish antiwar forces were personally attacked by the ADC, notably Svanstrom and lawyer-supporter Hans-Goran Franck. Svanstrom had not had much contact with the young men and so was not held in any particular affection by them. Franck, however, had been instrumental in processing almost all the early applications for asylum, and certain special legal matters pertaining to the deserters' rights in Sweden. He and his wife, Inger, furthermore, had befriended many of the men, who in turn felt real gratitude. The fact that Franck served as advocate for many other exile groups, notably the Greek community, the Gypsies and the Czechs, and that he was active in Amnesty International did not serve him well as against his role as a member of the Swedish Vietnam Committee. Membership in that committee was enough to condemn him. The word went out that Franck was not to be trusted. Yet many who knew the Francks reasoned that if they could not be trusted, no one could be. The instinct of those Americans who knew the Francks was to see them as decent humanitarians caught in a political bind. Friends of the Francks came to their defense.

* Mr. Svanstrom received the Soviet Union's Lenin Peace Prize in 1970. He is prominently associated with the Stockholm Conference for Peace in Vietnam.

A Force to be Reckoned With

In the midst of such discussion, the issue of political asylum, absolutely essential for all, came to be overshadowed by the internal dissension within the community. The parish out of bounds showed signs of being split right down the middle aisle before I even got there. In the background of this potential split lay both a personal and a political force. Michael Vale, an American translator fluent in a number of languages, had taken up residence first on the Continent, and later in Sweden. Vale is a committed socialist, thoroughly grounded in his politics and infused with a passion for hard work. In those months of 1968, man after man found his human and political identity through long raps with Mike Vale. There was no one who did not take him seriously. Many feared him, and some hated him. Some liked him, and still do.

A tough revolutionary who knows, as Trotsky himself declared, "It is not enough to seize the power—you have to hold it," Vale never let up in his goal of radicalizing the political consciousness of the men in their struggle to stand up to and overcome the oppressive experiences that dominated their lives. With his passionate devotion to the working-class make-up of most of the deserters, it is understandable that many of those men who had come from more middle-class backgrounds were turned off by him. A measure of his personality may be seen in the fact that I was assured by one member of the Swedish Vietnam Committee that he was indeed an agent in the employ of the U.S. government, and by an American that he was nothing more than "a political dilettante." I, personally, came to respect him and to regard his contribution as essential and helpful. If Michael Vale had not been on the scene in those early days, I doubt that a solid political base with clear positions could have developed in the exile community as a whole. Not only was the American Deserters Committee positively enabled by his presence, but his urging all the men on confirmed a sense of personal identity and consciousness in many fellows who did not see themselves getting involved politically.

Nevertheless, Vale could denounce a man or a group as counter-revolutionary and be believed. Naturally, those who did not see themselves as "the enemy" moved to oppose him. In a struggle for different leadership within the ADC in late October, 1968, the insurgents lost. Some, like John Toler, a former Green Beret Sergeant, had been among the most staunch supporters of the group. Though the fight was fought on procedural grounds, both personalities and politics were involved. It was inevitable, I believe, given all the circumstances (the group then numbered over 200) that an attempt would be made to form a new group. If you put two Americans in a room together for an hour, I often told the Swedes in interpreting the split, they will come out as two groups. (For all our madness, I think we Americans still take control over our destinies rather seriously. We just try too hard to take everyone else with us.) In Sweden, the result, for a time, was "The Underground Railway."

Workin' on the Railroad

TUR, as the Railway came to be known, thus organized itself for the primary purpose of "the general welfare of the deserter-resister community" in Sweden. Politically, their demands were indistinguishable from the ADC, except on the question of revolutionary struggle. TUR called for: (1) an immediate end to the war in Vietnam, (2) an end to all aggressions and imperialistic acts, (3) the control of America to be returned to the people, (4) immediate freedom for Huey Newton of the Black Panthers and all other black people, (5) complete amnesty for all deserters and draft resisters and (6) political asylum for all deserters and draft resisters in Sweden. In point of fact, most of the energies of TUR were expended on finding housing, jobs and schooling for their members and anyone who turned to them. Members of TUR also looked for personal help in working through their understanding of themselves, and with the assistance of an American psychologist, Dr. Robert Rommel, who was then on the staff of a Swedish Institute, a series of sensitivity training sessions were held.

Under the driving care of Lon McDaniel, an ex-Specialist 4 from Aberdeen, North Carolina and former ADC member (later reunited), TUR published its own newsletter, *The Internal Hemorrhage*, subtitled "Organ for American War Resisters in Sweden." When the word got out about TUR's newsletter, the ADC proceeded to publish its own sheet, *The Paper Grenade*. The effect was remarkable. On precisely the points that The Underground Railway had organized, the ADC was reorganizing. Apparently, there was a "third front" and it was in Sweden. With the government's announcement on February 21, 1969, of a new policy of "humanitarian asylum," the ADC was fully engaged in its campaign for full political asylum and for interpreting the question to Swedish supporters in an issue of the *Second Front Review* (in Swedish). After being in existence for about three months, TUR folded for lack of support. A few of the insurgents returned to the ADC, but by this time, a constant influx of new men meant that nearly half the number present in Sweden had not been involved in either ADC or TUR. The focus on new arrivals continued, officially with ADC and unofficially with many who were not in ADC, but who still accepted responsibility for orienting and guiding new men.

Another major concern surfaced at this time, with the increased number of men who were strung out on drugs. A medical service of sorts was established by Anne-Marie Rubin, a member of the Swedish young leftist group, the FNL-ers. Through it all, young Swedes like Miss Rubin, associated with the Front for National Liberation, supported the American deserters and resisters, openly raised the issues of the rights of the Vietnamese people and support for their struggle against the United States, and organized around the complacency of Swedish complicity with imperialism in any form. In particular, the work with Americans hooked on speed or LSD consisted of hearing out about ten or so fellows involved. An enormous number of hours were spent in trying to get certain fellows into hospitals or, if "cleaned out," back into school. FNL-ers also labored to get speaking engagements for the Americans in semiannual "American Deserters Weeks" in towns and cities throughout the country. Contacts were developed in these areas so that new men could eventually settle in areas outside Stockholm, notably Gothenburg, Uppsala and Malmo. During 1969 and into 1970 local groups of the ADC were activated and then slacked off in each of these three cities.

"It's Just Like a Barracks"

Soon after the February communiqué from Mr. Holmquist, the Minister of the Interior, another issue was laid in the political lap of the ADC. Gosta Broborg, head of refugee resettlement for the AMS (Labor Market Board), pushed ahead on plans to round up as many men as possible to place them in a "language camp" about eighty miles northeast of Stockholm in an isolated town called Österbybruk. The men were called to a meeting on April 1 in the Immigrants Information Office and told—they were never consulted—of the existence of the camp and of its various "advantages."

Mrs. Carillo advised the men that one-half million strangers had come to Sweden in the last thirty years, compared with the same number for all previous years of Swedish history. The men were told that they would not be forced to go to the camp but would be "encouraged" to do so. The camp was said to be "just like a barracks" where "you can come and go." Language classes would be conducted six hours a day, and a student would get 3 crowns (60¢) a day if he attended. All other expenses would be paid. The goal was said to be eventual placement in jobs or vocational training schools. At the same meeting, Mrs. Kristina Nystrom, who was later to be highly successful in reaching our men, was introduced as the new government social worker who would "help to learn more of the needs of the Americans living here."

Within the next several weeks, some fourteen men were advised when they went to the social bureau for their social help, or to the employment office to look for a job, that they would have to go to the camp. When they went to *Arbetsformedlingen* —the employment office—Mrs. Turberg told them they could no longer receive support for attending Swedish classes in Stockholm. To the men, this seemed like a real "messing over" by the bureaucrats. Clearly, Mrs. Carillo and Mrs. Nystrom were initially taken in by Mr. Broborg's presentation of the voluntary nature of the camp. The next issue of *The Paper Grenade* showed that the deserters were not. A cartoon of GI's lashing out at the American brass and Sweden's "big money boys" carried a caption: "This is not the Presidio:* This is the AMS camp near Uppsala. Stockade prisoners organize."

In a press conference in late April, I attacked the "psychological harassment" of the men by the Swedish bureaucracies. Thereafter, I was assured by certain officials that changes would be made. The point I tried to make then, and one I still believe to be crucial, is that Swedish policy toward the deserters is often contradictory, especially regarding middle-level hassles with labor and social bureau officials. Often many Swedes seemed to be playing games with these men as human beings. Caught in the crossfire of internal battles within Swedish politics and/or bureaucracies, the men were in no position to draw the fine distinctions essential to their survival. Specifically, my feeling was that Sweden wanted all the political credit for accepting the American war resisters, but little of the responsibility for job training, housing and schooling. The exceptions— notably the work of Mrs. Nystrom—made it possible for us to break through the red tape in many cases and be of some help. The Österbybruk camp, for example, was made voluntary at last, and continued to service some forty persons over a six-month period. Gradually the bitterness I felt toward Swedish policy in general gave way to a working skepticism that enabled us to do what we had to do without a lot of hassles.

---

* A reference to the Sixth Army stockade in San Francisco and the cases of the "Presidio 27," court-martialed for "mutiny" after a sit-down, convicted and sentenced. The judgments in these cases were overturned eighteen months later.

RITA and the Desertion Movement

About this time another development began to take up a good deal of discussion time within the inner circles of the ADC. One of the constant tensions within the movement, in the United States, has been the result of the desertion act, and the deserters themselves, being put down as apolitical. This was always less true in Europe than in the States, where much of the active-duty GI organizing was going on. In 1969, however, we saw a heavy increase in the load of cases that the panel of lawyers out of Paris had to handle on U.S. bases in Germany. This meant a necessary reconsideration of relationships with friends on those bases on the part of key members in the ADC.

The acronym for those GI's and their supporters, committed to working from within the bases, and primarily around issues of GI rights of protest, is RITA—Resisters Inside the Army. Earlier in 1968, there had been a considerable struggle on this question among those men who were in Paris. While Paris had become a haven for some of the deserters, it had also become "R and R" for resisters working inside the Army. By late 1969, it became necessary to forge some new ties with several key contacts, notably around Frankfurt, Germany.

The most critical political problem was to establish an understanding that would not oppose the RITA's and the deserters. A tendency to put down one or the other position had characterized some material in various publications. This could not be allowed to continue if the fundamental work of organizing the GI's in their common oppression was to be done. A first contingent of three persons was sent down from Stockholm to explore what could be done. Later, two returned and some others went south to Germany more or less permanently. In this second group was a bright young American woman married to one of the deserters. The couple had been a solid rock of superb organizing ability in Stockholm. (Her husband stayed in Stockholm.)

Fred Gardner, in an excellent article entitled "The Future of Desertion," referred to this tension in strategy at some length.

There has been considerable criticism of those who go to Canada by Resistance [civilian] spokesmen such as Joan Baez, and by organizers within the GI movement. I have even heard coffeehouse staff members speak bitterly about deserters, angry that they had not stuck around to circulate the petition (or whatever the current on-base organizing effort may have been).

Judging from the history of how armies fail, it appears that disintegration, not dissent, may characterize the final crisis. There has never been an army that fell apart through the exercise of civil liberties; but there have been some big ones cracked by mass desertion. As a tactic, desertion has the under-rated virtue of simplicity. It is the archetypal anti-war act.

We should not think of desertion, mechanically, as an alternative to on-base organizing; that's like saying the forehand is alternative to the backhand and therefore a tennis player should only rely on one. The fact is, desertion and dissent are two aspects of the same movement and re-inforce one another. It's not coincidence that the desertion rate shot up in the spring of 1968, just at the time that on-base organizing became widespread (and in the wake of the Tet offensive).*

My own impression is that a new unity has been discovered among those who continue to work with GI's in Europe. Gardner's major point seems to have been learned well, in the midst of the ongoing struggle for genuine freedom.

"Personal Work"

A good deal of simple human relations meanwhile took up most of my time—what used to be called, in evangelical Christian circles, "personal work." But I saw this as inseparable from the political organizing we tried to share in the overall community. Hard political work is unglamorous and often comes down to visiting someone in jail, or getting out a newsletter or answering the telephone fifty times a day. I saw growth among the deserters and resisters in this regard, as more men began to

* *Hard Times,* (formerly *MAYDAY*), a newspaper, No. 76, May 4–11, 1970.

see the necessity of taking people where they were as they first arrived, or at their own points of need, and building from there. Often we would find fellows who would say, "You know, I'm not political and I don't want to belong to any organization." And you'd find down beneath that what they thought was politics was no more than what passes for political activity—Democrat or Republican parties in the States. No one had ever helped them to interpret or to understand their own convictions in light of a larger, sustaining view of their world.

Much of our time was spent in trying to help these young men, and the women who were struggling along with them, to think things through. We sought not only to survive but, *with them*, to develop in creative ways. One instrument for this process was the family meal in our apartment in Solna. Largely without our being conscious of it, dinnertime became, within a month of our beginnings, the time of reflection, the time of celebration. Seldom did we have fewer than ten persons around the table. What we were doing, of course, was sharing in a para-eucharist, the fellowship meal important to both Jews and Christians. Often we had readings, sometimes from the Bible itself, more often from "contemporary epistles"—current social critique and even letters from home. The Hayes family, however, was under little illusion that it was always the company that folks came to share. Food on the table, and the prospect of a full stomach, were attractions enough.

Meanwhile in another apartment at Karlbergsvagen 52 in Stockholm, night after night was spent in similar fashion. There the headquarters for the ADC functioned for more than a year. New deserters were housed and more people were fed out of that place. In fact, around Stockholm at large, wherever two or three people got together, "rap sessions" would spontaneously develop. Paradoxically, all these meetings illustrated the independent spirit of their struggle. Depending upon one another quite strongly, they became together a kind of nylon cord of the human spirit. I was often in awe of them for showing this quality.

Their position is well illustrated by Herb Washington, a

twenty-seven-year-old black from Tacoma, Washington, and a
seven-year Army veteran. He told me that he knew nothing
about politics when he split. "I only knew what I *didn't* like—
the damn Army system. Now my work here [organizing the
fifty or so men in Malmö] has made me politically aware. I go
to Malcolm X or to Stokely and I read. Then I try to get others
to make the connections for themselves. But, sometimes they
just ask me, 'Man, what'd he say?' I've learned one thing
though. I would rather make a good run than a bad stand."

Joe Hill would like that. That's organizing.

chapter 5

PROFILING THE DESERTERS, PENTAGON STYLE

What Price AWOL?
Many servicemen who go AWOL are not aware of the seriouness of the act. AWOL is a serious offense, as much so as larceny, fraud or robbery.

Soldier Outlaw
If you go AWOL, notification that you are a fugitive or outlaw wanted by the Army is made to: your family—police in your hometown—sheriff of your county—FBI—Military Police—the Adjutant General in Washington—Commander of Army in which your home is located.

Birds of a Feather
As a prisoner, you will be locked up, guarded and watched. You will have placed yourself in and will be thought of as part of a group that includes:
    —Persons of low intelligence and poorly educated.
    —Mentally-emotionally unbalanced persons.
    —Criminals, alcoholics, deviates.
    —Un-American and unpatriotic soldiers.
    —Ignorant "know it alls" who say "I have nothing to
        lose."

—Department of the Army pamphlet

While the deserters guided themselves through the trails of exile, the forces of American military power were far from idle.

The Army, especially, was fighting back. More important by far, in a public relations sense, than the Army's agents in Germany and Stockholm, were the statements being made by prominently placed officers, in Germany and the Pentagon, about the deserters.

"Don't go AWOL," warned the Department of the Army in a pamphlet it rushed to print. "This thoughtless act" will brand a young man as a "criminal." Thoughtless or not, a lot of soldiers were ignoring the Army's warning. When they kept on ignoring it for thirty days or longer, the Army classified them as "deserters" or "military absentees." Regardless of their absence from post, however, these men were still considered the property of the United States. Ex-servicemen they were not. Deserters continued to be "in the service of their country," assigned to the information directorate of the Pentagon.

The Army's Study

One particular effort on the part of the Pentagon was published in the United States and featured in the papers of Stockholm. I had to deal with it. On April 14, 1969, the Pentagon released information from an Army study of 116 former soldiers who had deserted to Sweden. The Associated Press story by its military writer, Fred S. Hoffman, is quoted in its entirety as it came over the wire service in Stockholm.

ARMY DESERTERS

WASHINGTON, APRIL 14—Opposition to the Vietnam war motivated only a relatively small number of the American soldiers who have deserted to Sweden in recent years, according to an Army study.

An Army study of the 116 soldiers listed as deserters to Sweden says more defected because of disciplinary problems than as a protest to U.S. involvement in the Vietnam fighting.

The report said of the 116 cases, 56 soldiers deserted because of disciplinary problems, 39 defected because of opposition to the war and there were no known reasons for the remaining 21.

The study used the files of the 116 men to construct this profile of a typical Army deserter in Sweden:

> —He is a regular Army soldier, nearly 23 years old and has had three years of high school.

> —He is single, had no civilian occupation or skill, came from the more highly populated states, could not adjust to Army life, and was a disciplinary problem before he defected.

The document omitted the names of the individual defectors while summarizing the information from the files of each one of them.

Among the disciplinary problems, involving civilian and military offenses other than desertion, were repeated AWOL (absence without leave), drug abuse, indebtedness and stealing.

Of the 116 total, 92 were regular Army men, 23 were draftees and one was a reservist the Army said had deserted to avoid being called to active duty.

Fifty-nine had no civilian occupations, while 19 had been laborers, 12 had held clerical jobs, one was an attorney, one was an entertainer and one a ski instructor before military service.

Their age averaged 22.77 years, their education 11.2 years. Seventy-five went to high school, but 40 of them dropped out before graduation.

Fifteen others had a grammar school education while 22 went to college. However, 19 of the college men didn't finish.

The group includes 71 men who were single, 16 married, one divorced and the remainder listed as unknown.

On the same story, *Expressen*, a Stockholm paper that does not blush in print, carried the story of its man in Washington, Ulf Nilsson. Mr. Nilsson quoted Colonel Stevens, the Pentagon spokesman, as announcing to the Swedes: "We should like to tell the truth about the deserters in Sweden. The American deserters in Sweden are a sad lot." The Colonel is quoted as saying of the reasons for the study: "We made the research to pulverize the untruthful picture of the deserter as a young man of high ideals, who fled because he detested the war in Vietnam. The facts are that the overwhelming majority chose Sweden for quite other reasons. Most of them had difficulties in adapting in general." Mr. Nilsson's article emphasized, as did Mr. Hoffman's, the conclusion of the Pentagon that most of the men have never even been near Vietnam nor did they risk being sent to combat. "The deserter is a thief, a drug addict or a cop-out. According to the Pentagon," Mr. Nilsson qualified.

The most remarkable piece of information contained in the *Expressen* story, however, was the assertion of Colonel Stevens that the interviews had been obtained by the American Embassy in Stockholm by going through the unit records of the men and *with the assistance* of the Aliens Commission of the Government of Sweden. (Since July 1, 1969, the work of the former *Utlänningskommission* has been taken over by the *Invandraverket*, The Immigrants and Naturalization Board.) "That authority in Stockholm," said the Colonel, "has been very helpful."

An Embarrassing Revelation

This revelation caused quite a furor in Stockholm. Two newspapers editorialized about the possible complicity of Swedish officials with the Army study. In the afternoon paper, *Aftonbladet,* on April 17, Jan Myrdal, writer and author, the son of prominent parents, the sociologist Dr. Gunnar Myrdal and Mrs. Alva Myrdal, a minister for disarmament concerns in the Swedish cabinet, asked with pointed concern:

Has the Aliens Commission committed a crime?

The Pentagon has published a "research" about the Vietnam war resisters from the United States in Sweden. According to the press, the Pentagon has done this in order to "pulverize" the picture of the deserter.

According to Colonel Stevens of the Pentagon, the material has been gathered with the help of the United States Embassy in Stockholm.

According to the same sources, the Aliens Commission has been very helpful. This means that Colonel Stevens is accusing Swedish officials of crime against *brottsbalken* [the Swedish neutrality code of law] Section 19:9. For this crime they can be punished with prison up to two years. Colonel Stevens also accuses them of crime against *brottsbalken* 20:3. For this they can be punished with removal from office and prison up to one year.

It must be cleared up whether the colonel is lying or whether the officials have committed a crime. It must not be like the last time when the investigations take place after the big power nation that incites the criminal act loses a world war.*

Pressure was on the Swedish government, and the Aliens Commission in particular. Quickly, the Swedish authorities denied knowing anything about the report or having cooperated in any way with its compilation. No one seemed to know how the Embassy got its information, since for obvious reasons the deserters never give interviews to the American Embassy. If such material was available to the Americans at all, it had to have become available by way of the police interviews the men must give when they first seek political asylum and their residence and work permits. Had the police at some level been the culprit? Possible, but not likely in Sweden, at least not at this level. On these matters the police function purely as administrators. Interviews are sent on to the *Invandraverket* and processed entirely from there. It seemed more likely from other events, for example, statements of certain officials from time to time, that lower level bureaucrats in the Aliens Commission may have been involved without the knowledge of their superiors. The charges of Mr. Myrdal died for want of oxygen. The air surrounding the incident on the Swedish side was polluted but no one could seem to clear it up.

---

* A reference to Germany after World War II. Swedish authorities complied with German requests for extradition of Germans who sought exile in Sweden.

A Closer Look

Still the Pentagon charges had to be met. The occasion for my doing what I could came a week later. Since our arrival a number of Swedish and American reporters had been after me for a statement. I kept a practiced distance for as long as I could, wishing to be as confident of a good beginning relationship with our men as I could and as accurate in my analysis of the situation as time and discipline would permit. When the time came, I dealt with the Pentagon study at length. I also dealt with certain practices of the Swedish authorities which, I charged, amounted to a psychological harassment of the men.

Unfortunately, for reasons that have never been completely clear to me, the story carried in the States mentioned only the latter charge under the lead "Clergyman Assails Sweden's Handling of U.S. Deserters." (Associated Press, April 21, 1969.) An answer to the widely published Army deserter research has not been available to the American people until now.

Read the Associated Press story again now before you go on. See if you do not find the following inconsistencies.

1. The average age of the 116 former soldiers is said to be nearly twenty-three years, yet the report does not give their average length of military service. How, then, can they be characterized as "drop-outs?"

2. If many did not finish high school, nor many of those who began college finish (as I found is true), to what does the Army attribute their staying in the Army so long?

3. What are the actual figures of offenses in the military? The Associated Press story does not say.

4. If the deserter comes from "the more highly populated states," does he by implication come from the cities? It would be useful to know the Army's estimate of rural-town versus city backgrounds of the men.

5. How does the Army determine a man's actual motivation, for example, in relation to Vietnam? Did their command-

ing officers ask them why they were deserting as they left their bases?

6. If the Army did the research itself, as it claims, why did not the researchers make the announcement rather than the Pentagon press man? If the Embassy in Stockholm did the work, why was the report not released from Stockholm?

Points 1, 3 and 5 seem especially crucial to me. The government cannot have it both ways. Either the men have deserted after a relatively short experience in the military, and can thus correctly be called "drop-outs," or they are Regular Army. The government's own figures show that ninety-two of the 116, or 80 per cent of the men, were in fact Regular Army. Again, if they averaged twenty-two months of military service, according to records I have kept, or even eighteen months, or let us grant twelve months, how does the Army account for their staying with it for so long? If they showed a predilection for this kind of behavior in civilian life, would they not have cut out at their first or second opportunity?

Criminals? Misfits? or . . . What?

On the matter of the deserters' alleged criminality, the Associated Press carried only the charge without the Pentagon's figures. The figures released by Colonel Stevens show a rather different picture from what is charged. Of the 116, fifty-six or nearly 50 per cent are said to have been in trouble. It turns out that thirty-eight of these cases were AWOL charges, the very offense that led to the study! Thus only eighteen, or 15 per cent, are alleged to have committed a crime other than one so serious as to have required the expenditure of thousands of dollars and extensive administration to profile. Of these eighteen, nine were for drug use, "mainly marijuana," said Colonel Stevens. Six were said to have run away from big debts, and eight were convicted of stealing money. Apparently there was overlap somewhere, but no one, including Mr. Hoffman, the AP writer, pressed the Colonel on his figures. At worst, fourteen men of 116 were alleged to have been guilty of something worse than going AWOL or smoking "grass." "Pulverizing" the picture, indeed. These "criminals" turn out to be just about as criminal as all their buddies in Vietnam, if the extensive reporting on the attitudes of GI's there bears any resemblance at all to the facts.

In any case, I would refer the reader to the report of Mrs. Kristina Nystrom and Mr. Kjell Oberg of the *Statens Invandraverket*, which indicated in late 1969 that these men were indeed adapting to Swedish society, that better than 90 per cent were at work or school, that only seven were at that time serving prison sentences and that only twenty-two had ever served time in Sweden. And in all but two of these cases, drugs were involved.

The Pentagon report on the deserters in Sweden is important, however—important in a radically different way from what was no doubt intended. How many people reading the Associated Press story, *which carried none of the Pentagon's own statistics on the charge of criminality*, took it for the gospel truth? How many people questioned that report, questioned the propriety or even the possibility of the Pentagon determining whether a man was "idealistically" motivated against the war? How many people realized that a man cannot present himself to Swedish authorities without indicating the reason for his being in Sweden and his reason for deserting from the U.S. armed forces? Most importantly, how many people were prevented by this Pentagon casuistry from seeing these fellows as real human beings who had made real choices and who could never be reduced to a statistics pad in Washington?

Of course, the charge that the deserters are misfits is not confined to the Pentagon study. About two weeks before the release in Washington of the figures showing a rapidly increasing desertion rate, General Harley Moore, the provost marshal for U.S. Army forces in Europe was quoted from Heidelberg, Germany, as saying that the desertion rate had "leveled off to a nuisance thing." He said he believed that some of the deserters, but only a minority, were conscientiously objecting to the war and to the military system. The rest were "simply cheats and habitual trouble-makers" who did the military a favor by leaving.

"These kinds," said the general, "have been deserting the military since it began. And for the same reasons. They are debt-dodgers or just responsibility-dodgers." The general sounded a note remarkably similar to the charges of the Pentagon's report. General Moore spoke of his four thick files on the whereabouts of "his" deserters from 1967 to 1969. He took a kind of fatherly concern in the matter and said he knew where they were. "Sixty-eight are in Sweden; 19 in France; 5 in Holland; 3 each in Canada, England and Ireland; two in Switzerland; one each in Australia, Jordan, Norway and Scotland." About 100 in all. That was all, he said.

Congress Gets a Body Count

This would have been news to the Pentagon. The Army's Deputy Chief of Staff for Personnel, Lt. General A. O. Connor, was at that time preparing the figures for the Inouye Committee meeting in March. In June, considerably more of General Connor's findings were released after testimony before the House Appropriations Sub-Committee. Both the rate of desertions and the use of drugs in the Armed Forces were said to be on the rise. The following tables summarize that information. Note that the Department of Defense figures in Tables 1, 3 and 4 are based on a fiscal year ending June 30.

TABLE 1
NUMBER OF UNAUTHORIZED ABSENCES

	1967	1968	1969	1970
AWOL	134,668	155,536	217,000(est.)	228,797
Deserters (over 30 days)	40,227	53,352	73,121	89,088

TABLE 2
RATE OF INCREASE

	1968 (over 1967)	1969 (over 1967)	1970 (over 1967)
AWOL	15.5%	61%	70%
Deserters	33%	82%	121%

TABLE 3
TOTALS ACCORDING TO SERVICE BRANCH

	1968	1969	1970
Army	39,234	56,608	65,643
Navy	5,621	4,897	6,352
Marines	8,104	11,078	16,109
Air Force	393	538	984
TOTAL	53,352	73,121	89,088

TABLE 4
RATE OF DESERTION
(per 1,000 troops)

	W.W. II 1944	Korea 1953	Vietnam 1966	Vietnam 1970
Army	63.0	22.5*	14.7	52.3
Navy	3.0	8.7	9.1	9.9
Marines	6.9	29.6	16.1	59.6
Air Force	—	—	0.35	.8
TOTAL	72.9	60.8	40.25	122.6

* For the calendar year of 1952.

These tables reveal why General Connor was asked to testify before the House sub-committee. The general was testifying for the Army about two problem areas it has, AWOL-desertion and drugs. (Rates for drug use were said to be 8.9 persons charged per 1,000 troops in Vietnam compared with 5.2 persons per 1,000 troops worldwide.) One of the interesting things that comes out of a study of these figures is an answer to the often-asked question relating to desertion rates in the European theater in World War II. General Connor conceded that the figure for World War II was about sixty-three per 1,000 and pointed out that the figure of twenty-nine per 1,000 for the Vietnam war in 1968 was much lower. It was, however, "much higher than we would like to see it," said the General. It may be noted that the figure of twenty-nine relates only to the U.S. Army, and that when the rate of desertion for the Marines is included (much higher now than in World War II), the desertion rate for 1968 was about 60.5 as compared with 72.9 for all forces in World War II.

There is a further difference between the numbers of men going AWOL now and the men who went AWOL or deserted in World War II. It is in the number of combat-readied troops. Five times more men were combat-trained in World War II as compared with a combat-ready status for Vietnam of 500,000.

Of the 10,110,103 who were inducted [World War II] only 2,670,000 were trained for actual ground combat; and of these a very large number, believed to be as high as a million men, soon managed to escape combat by such devices as bad-conduct discharges, or self-inflicted wounds, or by being excused by psychiatrists for some form of mental insufficiency.

Among those who evaded combat were about forty thousand who were believed to have "taken off" or "bugged out" or "deserted before the enemy." Most of these were tried by lesser courts-martial and confined in the disciplinary training centers or dishonorably discharged. A total of 2,864, however, were tried by general courts-martial, and these received sentences of from twenty years to death.

And of the death sentences decreed by the general courts, forty-nine were approved by the what is known in military law as "the convening authority." . . . No deserter was actually shot except Private Slovik.*

An Eternal Dilemma

One might infer from the present desertion rate that if the government and the Pentagon had endeavored to get a declaration of war for Vietnam, instead of prosecuting the war under order of the chief executive, we would have had an answer to the question put to Walt Whitman in the last century: "Suppose they gave a war and nobody came?"

In a special interview which General Connor gave the editors of *U.S. News and World Report,*† he was asked how he accounted for the rapid increase in the desertion-AWOL rate over the past year. "We are getting more kooks into the Army, for one thing," he said. "We are getting more young men who are coming in undisciplined, the product of a society that trains them to resist authority." Questioned about why the Army training could not overcome this sort of thing, he alleged that "most of the desertions take place very early in the man's training. We do not experience this sort of thing in the trained soldier to any great extent." Nonetheless, the Pentagon has expressed satisfaction at the success of its Project 100,000, in which 246,000 "new standards" men were recruited from many nonwhites and whites formerly considered mentally or physically inferior.‡ So, then, the cause of desertion cannot be merely "the society that trains men to resist authority."

Still the charge may contain considerable truth. It is echoed often in the questions I am asked when I speak around the

* Huie, *The Execution of Private Slovik*, pp. 11–12.
† July 7, 1969.
‡ Report released January 26, 1970. Almost half of the 246,000 men, 49.3 per cent, were recruited from sixteen southern states, Puerto Rico and the District of Columbia.

country on campuses and in local communities. In a *New York Times* article by William Beecher, that newspaper's military affairs writer, another unnamed general is quoted as believing that "these young men, let's face it, are a reflection of the general permissiveness of our society."‡ One wonders whether this is good or bad. Presumably the goal of a free society is to increase to some extent the possibilities of "general permissiveness" for an ever-increasing number of members of that society. These spokesmen for the military honestly believe what they are saying, I have no doubt. Their feelings are shared by a great many genuinely concerned Americans. I would point out here that the men involved simply see it differently, as is understandable. For them, the military system that recruits them (more than 80 per cent of our armed forces are still recruited), or that drafts them to become trained professional killers in a war they do not understand against an enemy they do not know, is also revealing a good deal about the society that sanctions such a military. One does not hear from the generals about the brutalizing experience in today's action army, about the overflowing stockades, about training for criminal activities in Vietnam.

No, desertion is better seen as the eternal dilemma of individuals up against the wall of the community, in this case epitomized by the orders coming down from the brass. Every individual who says "No" breaks the chain of command, and that is very threatening indeed. Jean Jacques de Felice is a young Parisian lawyer who has defended many cases of French draft resisters since the Algerian war. Speaking of the Americans, he said, "American society fears and detests deserters because they are not only deserting from the Army but from the values of the society." In this sense, the generals have inadvertently felt the most sensitive pressure point in the desertion movement. It is not surprising that they (the brass) are unable to deal with it. It is beyond their comprehension that sizable numbers of young Americans could actually feel this way.

‡ "A Reflection of the General Permissiveness," March 16, 1969.

Thus, to conclude this discussion of the Pentagon's profiling of its rebels, we must look elsewhere for our understanding of these men. For one thing is missing from the official files: the heresies of their own experiences.

chapter 6

"FOR EXAMPLE . . ."

I have only one solution: to rise above this absurd drama
that others have staged round me. . . . What is needed is to
hold oneself, like a sliver, to the heart of the world, to inter-
rupt, if necessary, the rhythm of the world, to upset, if
necessary, the chain of command, but . . . to stand up to the
world.

—Frantz Fanon, *Black Skin, White Masks*

If the Army specifically, and the Pentagon generally, were
"fighting back," they were fighting a losing battle against the
actual experiences of the American GI's who were training for
and fighting on the battlefields of Southeast Asia. Young
Americans from 1965 to 1970 were living heresies. Taught to
fight clean, they were learning to fight dirty. Taught to live for
freedom, they were dying for tyranny. Somewhere in my theological training I learned that heresy is "the rebellion of a
truth forgotten against a truth remembered." Here, then, are
some stories of truth forgotten that have amounted to a "politics of experience," in the phrase of R. D. Laing, for many of
America's sons and brothers.

Bill and Ray

Bill and Ray were assigned to a Special Forces training unit
of the U.S. Army in Germany. For one part of their training
they were being taught counter-insurgency tactics, or how to

fight the guerrillas' own war. Then they were assigned for training to a unit of the West German Army. The purpose was to train the Americans in population control. The training was innocuous enough: how to build detention camps, how to account for the inmates, how to distinguish between civilians and prisoners-of-war. But this was too much for these soldiers. Bill told me, "It just blew my mind. I mean, like we were learning it all from the Germans; we were becoming today's Nazis. I couldn't take it, so I cut out of there as soon as I could."

Bill's buddy, Ray, after a short time AWOL in Sweden, decided to return to his unit before his thirty days were up. Bill stayed and became one more "military absentee." Bill says he will never go back. "I'd rather be a good American than a good German."

Chuck

Chuck tells me of his training in various methods of torture as part of his duty with the Special Forces. He was to be sent to Vietnam after learning "how to make prisoners talk." One method was particularly abhorrent to Chuck: the "helicopter method." In this procedure prisoners are taken up in American helicopters, dangled from the ship and then, if they do not talk, dropped to the ground in or around villages. Chuck split from his training unit in Germany and has now lived in Sweden for more than two years.

Mark

Mark, 22, from St. Paul and Marshall, Minnesota, was among the first men to follow the Intrepid Four out of Vietnam, and with the help of Beheiren, the Japanese antiwar organization, on to Sweden by way of the Soviet Union. (Edwin "Pappy" Arnett was in this group.) Mark's decision to desert occurred one day when he was out on patrol. "I saw my buddy shot beside me. That's what made me desert," he told me. "I could think of no good reason why he should die, why I should die, why any GI's should die in Vietnam."

During his tour of duty, Mark came to know several Vietnamese as human beings from encounters with them around the post and on patrol. One young Vietnamese who worked on base affected him deeply. He never did adjust after this to hearing the Vietnamese called "gooks" or "slant-eyed bastards."

After fourteen months in Sweden, Mark made plans to bring over his fiancée, Virginia, his hometown girlfriend. Virginia came in May and for two months the two of them debated their future. They had their problems. Mark is Jewish and Virginia is Roman Catholic. Virginia's parents opposed the marriage, partly because of the difference in their religious backgrounds, and partly, though they knew Mark, because of the uncertainty of Mark's future. The young couple resolved to go to Canada if they could, hoping that easier access to their parents would help. Mark began to make plans accordingly, including visits to the American Embassy. The deputy consul at the Embassy, Merle Arp, took an interest in Mark, and Mark took the opportunity of these visits to explore the possibility of a conscientious objector classification for himself.

On Sunday, July 27, as Mark and Virginia were in Arlanda airport, Mark was faced with the presence of Mr. Arp and four U.S. Marines. Mark was terrified and assumed the soldiers were planning to board the plane to Montreal, there to arrest him and return him to military authority. A series of quick phone calls were made, but nothing further occurred. Beyond Mr. Arp's greeting, no further move was made. Apparently, Mr. Arp was just showing, by means of an official escort, his concern for Mark.

In Canada, Mark and Virginia have married and are closer to both sets of parents, a major reason for their exchanging countries of exile. Mark has entered the University of Waterloo, and thus is about to fulfill a long-time dream of going on with his higher education. Eventually Mark hopes to "go into law." They seem to be very happy with the shape of their life together among the 80,000-plus American deserters and resisters who are some of the "new Canadians."

George

George, 25, from Evansville, Indiana, completed two years of college at Indiana University and received a teaching certificate in that state. He taught three semesters as a sixth-grade parochial schoolteacher before being called up by the draft. Faced by the latter prospect, he enlisted in the U.S. Navy, in which he served for twenty-one months before jumping ship in March, 1966, in Cannes, France. He spent some time in Paris where he met Chantal, a young Vietnamese woman and French citizen, whom he married. For a time they lived in Geneva before coming to Sweden in December, 1968.

George felt deeply opposed to the U.S. involvement in Southeast Asia. Yet he had not been there. In order to "face the music" he volunteered for naval service in waters off Vietnam. When it appeared that orders would come down for his ship actually to go to the Tonkin Gulf, his misgivings about the war were crystallized. He felt he could not be party to military service there at all.

In a letter he wrote to a friend in his hometown, he spoke of his feelings, especially regarding the friend's concern for George's isolation in exile in Sweden:

"My loneliness lies not in having severed old friendships, but in glancing about the world—Vietnam, Czechoslovakia, Cuba, Biafra—and feeling that none of my friends care. My loneliness was not created in the breaking of ties that bind me to my home, but in attempting to unite the ties that bind humanity. I find that my friends have other worries. My loneliness is their passivity, their blind acceptance of an amoral minority, their small world of egotistic problems and their freedom to continue in this rut."

George now studies sociology at the University of Uppsala, where he and Chantal and little Nathalie (born late in the revolutionary month of July, 1969) now make their home.

Michael

Michael, 25, is from Manhattan, New York City, one of the rare "big-city boys." After completing his B.A. in English from

New York University, he was drafted. He lasted nearly a year in the Army before receiving orders for Vietnam. At the time he was based at Fort Ord, California. While he was in basic training, he discovered himself to be conscientiously opposed to killing people. The nonviolent trigger for Mike was the practice at Fort Dix of jogging around the barracks and shouting "Kill . . . Kill . . . Kill" every time the left foot hit the ground. He applied for conscientious objector status and was turned down in Washington where all such appeals must be decided, regardless of any sympathy an officer may have for an individual's case. By this time, he was being shipped out and there was no time for appeal to a civilian court. At home in New York City, on leave, he got himself a passport. It was April, 1969. He could find little information on the situation in Sweden; he simply boarded an SAS flight to Stockholm. He expects now to develop a civilian hobby, which became the object of some military training— photography. He might have gone to Canada if he had known that country was open to deserters. He hopes to bring his fiancée over to Sweden soon.

Wayne

Wayne, 24, hails from Louisville, Kentucky, where his father is a professor at the Baptist Theological Seminary. He is a draft resister, rather than a deserter, and as such he is one of perhaps fifty men now living in Sweden because of similar convictions.

After graduation from Atherton High School in Louisville, he attended Centre College in Danville, Kentucky. After a year he went abroad to study German at the Universities of Vienna and Munich. While in Europe, he became quite interested in traveling, and made it to Sweden on a visit. On returning to the United States two years later, he believed he should not avoid the draft.

John Rayburn, a Louisville draft counselor who knew Wayne, says, "Wayne probably could have gotten a Fulbright scholarship or a job as a translator with an Embassy. But he turned these possibilities down because he felt if he allowed himself to take deferments he would be aiding, abetting and perpetuating the draft system."

Wayne was faced with the choice that still comes to all our male youth, bringing the war home to American families in a way that even television cannot. "When faced with the choice of taking human life unjustly or leaving my country, perhaps forever, I did not hesitate to choose the latter," Wayne says. "The most important concrete situation in the U.S. today is the draft. Men are called to kill unjustly in order to support profit-seeking government and businessmen. It is thus impossible to reconcile my own freedom and that of the Vietnamese people with any cooperation on my part with the U.S. Army. In Christian terms, every man has a soul. To take the life of a man whose soul is free is the worst of sins."

Wayne and his wife, Anne, who comes from Tennessee, now live outside Stockholm. Fluent in German, he is proceeding with graduate study at the University of Stockholm.

Bill

Bill is now 19. He comes from Baton Rouge, Louisiana. I met Bill when he had been out of the Army for only three months. We set him and his buddy up with an apartment, then went about hearing Bill "rap" about his story *and* his music. Bill plays the guitar well, the saxophone, trombone, clarinet, bassoon and horn fairly well. We had a bit of a shake-out on the possibility of getting all his instruments over from Baton Rouge. I was already a little famous—in Sweden and at home —for similar efforts with guitars, accordions and the like.

Bill dropped out of high school at the age of seventeen. His father is a section foreman for a railroad in Louisiana. His mother died when he was thirteen. "I and my daddy don't see eye to eye on quite a few things," he told an interviewer in Paris shortly after he had deserted. "So I enlisted to get away from home." He first thought the Army would be a good career. He made corporal in five months. Then he started changing, he says, and admits "that's a bad thing to do in the Army." He was being sent to noncommissioned officer school, where he was to be trained as a tank commander for Vietnam. "I was put in a leadership position, and the things you were being taught—what you say goes, no matter what. Right or wrong, you're responsible for all these men, and you tell them to do this and they *have* to do it. There's no reason for it. Some of the things that are done, I just don't agree with. You're taking a man and making a toy out of him, or a machine . . . just like a slave. I don't think it's right."

He began asking a lot of questions. Mostly he asked for reasons for doing what he was told he had to do. He felt more and more like a machine. When he would disagree with his superior he would be put on a detail. "They have choice people they'll put on them, and I was one of the choice of the choice." He was demoted to E-1, somewhat understandably. Meanwhile, he was putting some things together.

One experience crystallized his convictions. He was reading an Army paper about different aspects of communism. It read, "Why do the Communists have to feed propaganda to their people?" Then he looked down the hall and that was all he saw —propaganda. His mind ranged on. "Why do the Communists have to build walls to keep their people in?" He looked out the window and saw a big wall going around the base. And the guards. He began to feel, and says to this date, that the Army was just like Communism. "Everything I've been taught about Communism in school *is* the Army," he told me and any others who would listen. When I tried to make a distinction between militarism, fascism and communism (small "c" variety), I lost him. It was a political line that I heard occasionally from other men, but never did it come through more sharply than with Bill.

He had gone AWOL once in the States, but he never intended desertion then. He was in Germany when that happened. The comparison between the Army and Communism was sharpened while he was there. He began to believe that the United States was denying the rights of the Vietnamese the way it was denying the rights of the line GI. He saw the war then as immoral and illegal. When that dawned upon him, he decided he'd better act. First he thought he should try to put up with it; get it over and go home. Then he felt he could not go along any more. "America's going to fall under its own weight because of the way it's run," he said later. "America is becoming more a dictatorship than a democracy."

Bill was consistent about his beliefs. He split on his own and went to France. Early on there he was picked out by "an admitted Communist" who wanted "to destroy everything," Bill said. When he came to Sweden he told me he wanted to have nothing to do with people who would destroy freedom. He was referring to what he believed to be true about some other deserters, and about the Swedes. He has come off the edge of his youthful pride on this point but not to the point of losing his convictions. He intends to finish his schooling and go on for a music degree in Sweden.

He told me that he had no regrets about deserting. He wished he had done it sooner. To an interviewer, he made the following statement. It is a fairly typical answer to the average American's fear that deserters are, in fact, cowards.

"I think if a man has guts enough to tell the whole nation to kiss it, he's anything but a coward. I don't think a deserter is a coward, because he's denouncing his home and his nation and his family and everything he's ever known and lived for, for his freedom. I don't think that is anywhere near cowardice. No, I'm not a traitor. I'm just a political exile. I'd suggest that people who think me a traitor look that word up in a dictionary and find out what the word means."

"Buz"

"Buz," 20, grew up in Quincy and Braintree, Massachusetts. Six months after graduation from high school, his name came up in the draft and so he enlisted "to get a better deal." That was in January, 1967. He took his basic training at Fort Gordon, Georgia, and his Advanced Individual Training (AIT) at

Fort Knox, Kentucky. Eight months after his induction, Buz was ordered to Vietnam where he was stationed with the First Squadron, Twelfth Cavalry. He was a long way from Braintree and his Italian-American home. Buz drove a tank in Vietnam. He was then eighteen years old.

"I went on shift at four A.M. one morning," he told me, "and at five A.M. the V.C. started an attack on us. Vietnam was such a rotten place. I am still sick from thinking about all the killing I did. I remember the Cong's face when I killed him. I wanted to vomit. I hate myself for doing it. All I ask myself is, Why? Why? Why did I do it? I wish that I knew."

After the battle was over, Buz went to his commanding officer and told him that he wasn't going to kill any more "Cong." And no one else, he said, if he could help it. The CO told him to go and see a "shrink" the next day. When Buz went over to the psychiatrist, he went by way of "Alice's Restaurant." He sang a few bars of the song as he tried to leave the captain's office. Two medics grabbed him and locked him up for two weeks' "observation." After this temporary confinement, Buz was given orders to Germany. Sometime during that period in the stockade he decided he had had it with the action army. As I met him, he was still shaking his head over the prospect of getting behind that tank and those guns and "remembering the Cong's face."

He planned to desert from his post in Germany. He had met an English girl in Germany, and they were going to Sweden together. In January, 1969, she was killed in an automobile accident on a highway outside London. Buz was now in bad shape. He made it three more months until on May 6, 1969 he went to his commanding officer and told his story. "Buz" played it straight, down to telling his CO of the planned desertion. The colonel was so affected that he asked Buz how much money he had. Before Buz could answer, this officer of the U.S. Army laid on his desk $100. Then the officer offered Buz a ride for the fifty kilometers to the Autobahn. I found myself also affected by this story, and what pleased me most is that Buz held no thought of having "conned" his CO. As far as Buz was concerned his case had merit, and the officer was good enough to recognize it.

The new deserter went on to England to visit his girl's grave and stayed for two days. He then traveled and worked where he could about England, sleeping in cow pastures, in Hyde Park, in vacated buildings. In Hyde Park, he met some people who helped him with his papers and gave him enough money for passage to Sweden. He told me that in London, "I met with some Members of Parliament as a deserter to discuss the chance of deserters getting asylum in England. And I met with some other lords and ladies to discuss the same."

On July 18, 1969, at ten P.M., he arrived in Sweden. Buz remembers it well. He kept a diary of his journey into exile. "Freedom at last!" he wrote that night. "We're in Sweden now —on the train for Stockholm. I feel at the top of the world. My new home, my new country. May I be happy here." He reflected later that he thought his only problem would be the language barrier, but that this would be compensated by the fact that "people take me for a Swede." This, in spite of his dark hair. "I will say what I feel," he told himself more than others; "I am home at last." His hopes were set down briefly on arrival in Stockholm. "Nobody met us at the train," he said, "and we were supposed to have someone there from the ADC (American Deserters Committee). But we had the wrong address. We finally got in touch with the ADC. We made it."

Buz has completed his initial language study and now works for a firm that makes radio and TV parts. He is living about 100 miles south of Stockholm. He called himself "ex-Spec 5 Buz." Lately, he has dropped the "ex-Spec 5."

Walter*

"I was born in New Hampshire. My father was a technician in the submarine base there, and by the way built the sub-

---

* From a booklet, *American Deserters*, published by War Resisters' International. Avaiable from WRI, 339 Lafayette Street, New York, New York 10012.

marine *Thresher*, which sank not too long ago. I was an illegitimate child—my parents were not married—which I never found out till later from a half-brother who instead of saying 'Hello, how are you?' said 'Hey! You are an illegitimate child'—which kind of hit me the wrong way.

"My mother worked in a drugstore in Portsmouth. When I was four we moved to New York City where we lived in a basement apartment, $17 a week. She spoiled me. I went to a Catholic school. My mother was sick with cancer. She didn't know it. At one time I lived with my half-sister in Massachusetts with her four children and husband, who were fairly well off and still are. At about one o'clock Easter Sunday morning my sister came back home, supposedly having visited my mother in the hospital. She told me that my mother died four days previously and was buried. That was a shock—finding out that your mother has been dead four days and you're 200 miles away from her. You don't know where she is buried, you don't know what happened. So it was a very, very sad thing. I hope nobody has to experience it.

"My sister sent me away to a camp for a whole summer. I was supposed to stay there only for two weeks, but thank goodness I liked the camp. She took me there the following summer and I learned arts and crafts there, learned to swim and I enjoyed it. Then my other half-sister came from New Jersey and told me that I was to go to a foster home the same afternoon. That shook the shit out of me. I was to leave my sister and the school where I was involved in the band and the music at the time. I was 13 and I enjoyed it there.

"I was in my first foster home three hours. All I remember is 'get out of here. I don't like it. I want to go some place.' A social worker came one snowy night and took me to another foster home. When I was there something very confusing happened, and I ran away. It just went on, from one foster home to another. I got beaten up here and there. Finally when I ran away to Alaska they caught me and sent me with a policeman all the way back to New York. I got away from the police and ran away to California. They picked me up again and said 'you're going to jail, kid, because you're a habitual runaway.'

"I was sent to reform school, where I stole the cottage-master's car and went to New Jersey. Some cop picked me up and put me in state police barracks, where you shine boots and wash dishes. I decided to take a state police motorcycle for a ride at three in the morning. They got me for that. The parole officers came and said, 'Aha! We are sending you back to the reform school—violation of parole—you broke too many dishes.' I went upstairs, packed my bags and decided to search for my father whom I found about three weeks later in Virginia. He did some sneaky talking over the telephone and tricked me into going back to Massachusetts and turned me in by putting me up in a hotel and having two policemen come to the door next day.

"When I was 16 I joined the Army under a false name and under a false age. During this time in the Army I had gone AWOL twice and been in Vietnam for three months, after which they had found out my real name and pulled me right out of Vietnam and sent me all the way to Fort Jackson, and put me in the stockade. When I was in Vietnam, I didn't understand what my function was. I repaired runways and went out on a couple of patrols. I was 17 at the time but the army thought I was 22. I didn't realize why I was out there shooting, etc. But I knew that what I was doing was wrong because I had been fired at and I have never fired back in 'the point' of the enemy for some strange reasons. I had always lain down on the ground, just stuck my helmet over my head and hugged that dear old ground. I didn't hit anybody. God knows. I had no idea what the situation was like in Vietnam. The Army told me to go there and there I was. I could not tell them 'I don't want to go,' especially in my situation where I was lying about all this. I never realized that I could get a Purple Heart.

"The person's name I used was in the Navy and evidently he had been killed in Vietnam. . . . They sent me to the stockade. I was put in 'the box.' I was there in shorts and a tee shirt up along with four other boys and when they called out my name I was over the third fence. One of the boys didn't make it. He fell between fences and got caught. I had made it for a day, but was caught by a helicopter, and sent back to the stockade. I was put in 'the box.' I was there in shorts and a tee shirt all the time and was fed, I don't know, 133 calories or 33 a day. All I remember is I had a tray of dried corn flakes, no bread, milk, sugar or anything. For lunch it was some kind of raw vegetables, a piece of celery and carrot, and at night I think it was a bowl of water and some kind of cookie or something. This went on for ten days. I was hosed down every day except two days, I think, because either I was so weak or when the officer came I refused to stand to attention. I really can't remember if I refused or whether I just couldn't do it because I was so weak.

"After that they let me out of the box and came up with some law under which I was put in the casual company, on KP for 18 days. KP is terrible. It's like 14/16 hours a day washing pots and pans and I always got stuck on pots and pans. So I decided 'No, I think I'll take a vacation.' I hitch-hiked around North America and Mexico; stowed away in a boat to Newfoundland, etc. I was working for a chicken supplier when one night I drove away with their car and went to Denver, the place I had enlisted in the Army three years before. There I met the psychologist who offered me a place to stay and a job at the Denver Mental Health Centre, giving all those tests to people who took drugs. This went on for about a week and I decided 'Well this can't go on forever. They're going to catch me for the car and I will be drafted.'

"I decided to join the Army. I falsified the statement 'have you ever had any prior service.' I said 'no.' They signed me up for the military police and I was sent to Fort Bliss where I took the basic training all over again. But when the security clearance came back they called me, 'O.K., Mr. ——, we've found out about you.'

"I thought, 'Ah. This is wrong that they are all out to get me. They are going to screw my future up.' The Company Commander came—20 years old, about six months older than I was, '——, I hear you are going AWOL tonight?' 'Me, Sir? No, Sir. I want to stay in the Army and be a lifer.' He was afraid of me because I had taken a swing at him before, which was kind of under cover and nobody ever said anything about it. But he never did anything, because there was a Lieutenant Colonel who was in my favor. They wanted to see me be a lifer obviously; I was very good military material.

"Anyway, I said 'no,' so he went home. But they put a one-hour check on me. A staff on duty came there about 11:30 and checked on my bed. At 11:31 I was downstairs and a minute later phoning for a cab. At two minutes to twelve midnight I had bought a ticket to Boston. I was in civilian clothes. I went to New York and then was given a lift to Canada by a girl. I went through the customs, went to a Negro professor, an American, who gave me the money to proceed to Sweden."

Walter recently received his Swedish licence to drive a taxi, which he has managed to do thus far without cracking up, either his car or himself.

Terry

Terry is 23, and was born and raised in Memphis, Tennessee. He comes from "an average-size Negro American family" of three brothers and two sisters.

Soon after he graduated from high school in 1966, he received the order from his selective service board to report for a physical. He then received a second letter, which gave him the choice of volunteering or being drafted. Under these circumstances he was inducted "voluntarily" into the U.S. Marines.

"In training I was taught the old military way, do now and ask questions later," he told a questioner. "I had somewhat of a head start on most of the fellows because of my previous training in high school. I had been a captain in the National Defense Cadet Corps. Therefore, on entering the Marines I was already an expert rifleman. But on becoming a Marine the training was very, very hard. Day in and day out the word 'kill' was constantly pounded into our heads. We were taught to uphold the long traditional history of the Marines as being the best America had to offer."

He received orders for Vietnam in May, 1966, and served in combat from June until December, 1967. He felt it was an honor to "serve my country." "I was told the war is for freedom." He was with the First Battalion, First Marine Division, Bravo Company. His unit was filled with many young men, all between eighteen and twenty-one. His commanding officer, says Terry, was out for revenge after losing a brother in battle. Within two weeks of this new CO's command the men were turned into "a mob of blood-hungry animals."

In December, his unit was on a thirty-day duty near Con Thien. "On December 15, my company was on patrol when we ran into a large force of NVA. Before we could move out, the enemy spotted us, forcing us to fight. My platoon was then cut off from the rest of the company. The enemy laid a perfect ambush, which sent the men tumbling to the ground. Only two of us were able to get away." He heard the shout of his lieutenant calling his name. Terry rushed out to pick up the wounded officer. The enemy shot the officer even as he was wounded but did not shoot at Terry. "The enemy had a clear view of me," says Terry, "and could have taken my life very easily. But he didn't. Why?" The incident had a profound effect on the black Marine. He is convinced that he did not receive fire because he, like "the enemy," was a man of color.

Later that day, the twenty-seventh of a thirty-day stint, he was hit and hurt badly. He and a buddy were left behind as the tanks retreated, while jets began to shell the area. After three hours a company came in to get them. It was to be his last moment on the battlefield of Vietnam. He was transferred first to Cam Ranh Bay where President Johnson and Field Marshal Ky awarded him a purple heart for his battlefield wounds. His mother was to see him on television as part of the coverage of the presidential visit and thus to learn for the first time that he had been wounded.

With multiple shrapnel wounds Terry was paralyzed in both legs and his right arm. He was transferred to an Army hospital in Yokohama, Japan. He considered his position in the care of the U.S. Army something of an indignity. He remembers that he would rise in the mornings to sing the Marine hymn to let the nurses and interns know "where it was at." When the *Stars and Stripes* would arrive he would check for the Army casualties and announce to his ward that the Army casualties were so high that the Marines were having to fight the whole damn war themselves. When he found that two Army EM's in the ward, one with a slipped disc and one with a broken ankle, were victims of little more than a game of football, he laid it on even thicker. Terry rather "dug" the hospital scene.

Meanwhile, he became more mobile through physical therapy, enough at least to be permitted leave from the hospital. He met a Japanese girl and struck up a friendship, later a love, for her. She was strongly opposed to the war, and Terry just as strongly spoke up for "the great United States" and "how we never did nothing wrong." Back at the hospital, on March 6, a doctor gave Terry "the word." "You're in great shape," said the physician. "A-class. I think we're going to send you back." To Terry, that was a very low blow. Already his parents expected him; he was down to that last phone call before coming home. Now it was all turned around. He was going back to "the Nam."

Terry's new girlfriend yelped when she heard about the doctor's decision. "You're going to get killed," she said. Terry told her he was going back and added "Charlie can't kill me." The girl asked Terry to desert. Terry really didn't understand. He heard the word "deserter" and said "it was Greek" to him. He reported to his jumping-off spot, a nearby Air Force base. Boarding the bus on the way he met a friend from his unit who told Terry of the rising casualties in Vietnam and that, meanwhile, Terry had been nominated for a Bronze Star.

At the air base, two white marines were talking through Terry who was wedged between them, as they waited for the plane to appear. Finally, one asked to get in front of Terry so that the two buddies could rap better. When the plane arrived, Terry discovered that he had been bumped, there being no space left for the next one in line.

Again the Japanese girl—her name was Chocko—tried to persuade Terry to desert. This time around some things began to sink in. He remembers that he was "thinking too much." About racist things. About why he was so low in rank. About how maybe "the Man wanted to finish me off." He couldn't get over being sent back to the battlefield after having received a Purple Heart and then a Bronze Star.

The next day at the airport all flights for Okinawa were canceled. Terry had his second reprieve. This one took. "That night we had a big party in Yokohama. Sam had had me balancing. I'd been debating with myself. My mind was finally set one way. It would have been set the other way if I'd boarded one of those planes."

For better than a month, Terry stayed with Chocko underground. In circumstances that are not very different from the many GI's deserting two years later from "R and R" tours in Japan, another GI—a nondeserter—brought him supplies and daily news. (The deserter is often aided and abetted by his GI buddies, even though they are not about to split themselves.) On one occasion Terry went out at night only to discover that a member of the shore patrol lived across the road. Always there was the terror of being found out. His GI friend reminded him of CID agents in the neighborhood. Terry became more terrified by night and more secluded by day. He decided to make a move. He had left his clothes at the airport, so he asked a friend to recover them—no problem, according to the friend. Then the friend handed Terry a card. It was a card from

Beheiren, which before the development of the JATEC (Japanese Technical Committee) was *the* organization that had aided the Intrepid Four and many others.

Terry refers to his subsequent escape from Japan and "the Man" as "the great historic voyage." I talked at length with him and with his buddies about their long journey. The tales that are told can match any cloak-and-dagger novel ever written. Within Japan alone there was a succession of auto switches and code word exchanges. In Hiroshima, Terry met and was questioned by the head of Beheiren. It was standard operating procedure, but Terry did not know that. Was Terry fleeing from a crime? Was he aware of the danger? Did he know the risk of desertion? Apparently Terry passed the test of the Japanese underground but not before being warned that he must make up his own mind, carefully.

Terry had made up his mind. He said goodbye to Chocko and was on his way. Weeks into his desertion he began to feel guilty. He told me on one occasion that he thought in a way it was too easy. I asked him what he meant. He said the people were so good and kind, and even though the war was behind him he felt like it should be a battle to desert. He was to find the battle ahead. It was his "R and R" that had been extended.

While staying with a priest in Hammatsu, Terry was awakened abruptly one day with the words, "They shot the king." "What king? I got no king," Terry remembers saying clearly. The Japanese cleric motioned Terry to look at the television set. It was April 4, 1968, and the news had come of Martin Luther King's assassination. "There were the streets of Memphis, my own hometown. I knew right then I wasn't ever going to give myself up. If I did, Sam would beat me up and send me back to 'Nam. Sam was killing my brothers and he could go straight to hell."

For Terry, his next combat zone was to be the very strange one of Stockholm, Sweden. He is winning the battle. You see him round the town and working now for IKEA, the large department store south of the city. And when you see him, you won't miss his black beret. He wants the Swedish kids who live around him to know that black is very beautiful and that "black power" stands for more than some ghetto burnings those kids may have seen on TV. Terry is going "right on."

chapter 7

OPEN LETTER TO A SOMETIME CLOSED MIND

He who can give light to the hidden
May alone speak of victories.
He who can come to his own formulation
Shall be found to assume mastery
Over the roads which lead
On the whole human event.

The hour of love and dignity and peace
Is surely not dead.
With more splendor than these sombre lives
The gates within us
Open on the brilliant gardens of the sun.
Then do these inscrutable soldiers rise upward,
Nourished and flowering
On the battleships of the Unseen. For Victory,
Unlike the sponsored madness in these undertakings,
Is not diminished by what is mortal; but on its peaks
Grows until the dark caverns are alight
With the ordained radiance of all mankind.

—Kenneth Patchen, *The Climate of War**

In dealing with the American public I was constantly tempted to defend the deserters, especially against the Pentagon charges. I had to learn to resist that temptation. I found that it is

* From *Collected Poems*, copyright © 1942 by Kenneth Patchen. Reprinted by permission of New Directions Publishing Corp.

precisely their vulnerability, or in usage more common today, their being "up front," that makes them humanly interesting. Give them a chance to speak and they will authenticate themselves.

Look magazine carried a story, "Protest in the Ranks," October 15, 1968, and featured some of the American deserters in Stockholm. The former employer of Steve, one of the men featured in the *Look* story, read it, called up his parents, and then wrote a letter to Steve, who responded with a letter of his own.

Steve's parents live in Flushing, New York, and his father is a tailor in Manhattan. The family name is omitted to insure a respect for their privacy. One of Steve's greatest concerns since his act of desertion in the spring of 1968 has been the reaction of his parents. His remarks about this concern are instructive, for it is a concern shared by a great many of the men.

"It's very difficult, it has been and is now, to communicate to them. It's something I couldn't grasp myself before I enlisted. It's very hard to recreate the emotions you have when it is something taking place in you. It's very hard to recreate that when you are not living through it. It was very hard to bring my parents to the circumstances I was in, to the emotions that I had at the time. To try to bring them in to all these areas is something that I have just about been frustrated in doing. As hard as it is to communicate to them, that's how hard it is to communicate to the American people in general. About what it's like, what leads you to do it, and what kind of emotions you have. My parents kind of accepted it on the basis that I believed in it, and if I believed in it as strongly as I did, then to do it was my only alternative."

December 27th, 1968

Dear Steve,

On a recent visit to our New York office, I learned much to my distress and sorrow your incident of leaving the United States Army and venturing into asylum in Stockholm.

I assumed the privilege of telephoning your home for possible further information and spoke to your sweet mother, whose voice of despair registered an appreciative and yet anguished tone to my call.

I am sure you know of my personal interest in you. My admiration for you as a person and the promise of great potential you constantly displayed as a human being, as well as a business man, always reflected the makings of a MAN with great attributes. By that I mean, you always appeared to have the ability and stability of facing adversities and unpleasantness, if and when they might appear, without losing the common human touch of recognizing REALITIES in this world do *EXIST* and they're not always to our liking, but must be part of our responsibilities!

I don't know what possessed you to do what you and your friends chose to do. Least of all shall I criticize and/or condemn you. Your motivations at the time, I am sure, seemed real and just. However Steve, as your friend and still employer, I urge you to reflect upon your past decision in its true and proper perspective.

You *are* an AMERICAN. This is *your* Country. It's the *home* of your *parents*, your friends and your *relatives*. This is *our* Government. It's the best in the world, *and*, RIGHT or WRONG, its decisions are our commands and they must be respected and obeyed.

Can you imagine Steve, the chaos if *ALL* Americans disobeyed the Laws of the Land and the decisions of our Government? DISAGREE, you can . . . DISSENT is your American privilege . . . DISOBEY . . . DESERT . . . REVOLT is Anarchy in the making.

Reflect for another moment Steve . . . . I am sure your Mother and Father and/or their parents, came to the United States because of the many opportunities and *FREEDOMS* our great Country afforded them. Freedoms and opportunities *NOT* available from whence they came. Look over your shoulder and reflect upon NAZI Germany, Communist Russia, China, Czechoslovakia . . . and yes . . . sixty miles from our Florida shores into Castro's Cuba etc., and visualize *ALL* the hurt and deprivations suffered by their people because of their form of Government. The daily Freedom Flights from Cuba are still crowded by humans who untiringly leave HOME . . . FAMILY, FORTUNE and FRIENDS . . . FOR FREEDOM in the true sense of the word!

Thank GOD, here in America, if we don't like what our Law Makers are doing and/or the Policies they formulate, we can vote them *out* of office every four or six years, and vote *in* those who

convey the WILL of the MAJORITY. That's a Great, Great freedom and privilege scarcely found anywhere else in the world.

It takes a BIG man to face the realities of life with which he
disagrees and still abides by them because they represent the laws
of the land. The will of the majority must ALWAYS prevail if we
are to remain free!!!

I didn't mean to get on a soap box and preach to you. My interest and admiration for you, dictated the content and the mean-
fulness (sic) of this letter.

Reflect upon it . . . correct it if you wish, then think of your future . . . your home . . . your family . . . your Country. Mentally
and morally honest men of stature usually take stock of themselves
in true reflection for their own honest well being.

It takes such a MAN to recognize his shortcomings admit to his
mistakes, and . . . it takes an even BIGGER man to *correct* same
in the face of adversities.

I assume the time element and the distance for corrective action,
if any is to be taken, is the nearest telephone booth, the cost, ten
cents in American money, and the source, the nearest American
Embassy.

America is our home . . . yours and mine! Come back to it. I
value you as a friend . . . . If I can be of any assistance in any
possible way for you to accomplish any corrective action you may
choose to make, I'm at your service.

The gang at ——— join me in this message to you.

Sincerely,

January 10, 1969

Dear ———,

I received your letter several days ago and was both shocked and
moved. The fact that you have taken the time to phone my mother
and to sit down and write your feelings in relation to me and my
present position in a personal letter is ever so gratifying to me. If
we never speak to one another again I still shall remember you
for the sincere interest and concern you have shown.

You spent much time talking of the greatness and comparative
freedoms that our country offers. This was unnecessary as I believe everything you said to be true. I, contrary to what you be-

lieved, did not leave the Army to protest against what is America today. Mine was a much more naive and innocent motivation. It stemmed, to be painfully honest, from fear. Fear turning to confusion, then to panic. Fear, not based entirely on my own well being, but fear also of having to kill other human beings. The country is not the cause. Nor even the World of wars that exists today. Rather it is my own uncontrollable fear of soldiering, of killing, of seeing life, the holy spirit that each and every man is, spilled and spattered in open wounds on some battlefield.

I spent four months in an Infantry unit in Germany before coming here. There I was taught how to fight with a rifle and protect our country. I couldn't even train to kill. I was sick there and alone because I was different. Most of the Americans in the Army accept soldiering as a job they must do as men. To fear it is not to be a man. I hated my fear and disgust of killing there. I hated it because I was treated as a man without manhood by the soldiers all around me. They do not see a man's life in the same perspective. To them killing an enemy is a masculine reality, a man's job, an American's privilege.

As I became aware of how hard it was for me to rationalize and understand sometimes the need for killing, as a soldier I began to feel naked. I knew I was there training to go to a war presently raging in Vietnam and realized I could not go there in the state of mind I was in. I would be killed or what's worse cause someone else to be killed. I then in hope of finding courage began to try to get the information which I hoped would teach me to hate the enemy in Vietnam. To give me reason to kill, as my fellow soldiers seemed to possess.

I spoke with the Chaplain (a foolish place to look for a reason to kill), I spoke with my Commanding Officer, I read literature, I talked and I searched. But I could not find what even the government can't seem to give the people at this time, a concrete reason to hate the Vietnamese enough to kill them. I began to get panicky, with no one to communicate with. It was all happening to me alone, in a place that was the furthest I had ever been from home. One week after receiving my orders for Vietnam I came to Sweden. Even further from my home. I came here confused and frightened and found a few others the same. Together we talked and tried to reassure ourselves that we were not the criminals that our possible five year sentences told us we were. I look for people to understand every place I go so that maybe they will help me to understand what has happened to me. But I'm still very much alone.

You spoke about me coming home in your letter. At this time there is the one place I know I would not be alone and wish very deeply I could be there. You spoke about the anguish and despair of my mother. I read that in letters every day. My father's are even worse. If I went home I wouldn't have to read those letters any-more. I wouldn't have to know that my mother and father feel those letters. For with me I would bring comfort for them. I don't have to be told that my home needs me. No more than I have to be told I need my home. But to go there now would mean to go back to the Army. At best back to the soldiering, back to Vietnam. At worse to a soldiers prison in Leavenworth to be punished by soldiers for not being able to be a soldier. Maybe after a year or two in prison I could be made into a soldier, that's probably what I fear most. I don't know. I'm scared and confused and very much alone and it looks like I must stay that way, or risk being worse. I'm fighting for my very life but I don't know who to struggle with. If only I could kill without hating. If only I could respect a soldier who does.

I don't have very much more to say. It has been very uncomfort-able for me to write what I have written so far. I wish I could say it all better, but I'm handicapped by my own doubts. What will I do? For the moment just wait in hope of some compassion and under-standing from my country and the amnesty that might come with it. Or for my own self-guilt to make me believe I must accept what punishments await me.

You offered in your letter to help me accomplish any corrective action I may choose to make. I believe you really meant that. If corrective action means going back to the Army, back to soldiering, I fear the only way you or anybody else could help me, right now, is to make me mentally and morally capable of doing just that. Something I could not make myself capable of doing to the point of being here. Maybe someday I will change and will not have to suffer nor cause the suffering that I do now. Maybe someday yet I will be a soldier. Or maybe someday I will be able to come home and just be a human being, a son to my parents, a friend to my friends, an American to other Americans. I hope that day comes someday, with all my heart, for that's all I've ever wanted to be.

Thank you for your concern, it's help in itself, and you yourself as a person have become through it another wonderful thing I've been made aware of I've lost behind.

Very sincerely,
Steve

January 30th, 1969

Dear Steve,

Your recent letter moved me so, that I took the privilege of forwarding a copy of it to *Look* Magazine, together with a copy of my letter, for their readers' edification.

I frankly resented the *Look* Magazine story and the pictures that appeared with it. Your letter was full of humanizing thoughts and beautiful moral expressions of justification that I wanted *them* to know, that in your mind, and undoubtedly in the minds of your associates, the motivations behind your actions were basic and fundamental before the eyes of any ordinary human.

Steve, I was very, very impressed with the contents of your letter, and as far as I am concerned it took a hell of a lot more guts on your part to stand by your beliefs than it would have taken for you to put them behind you and shoulder a gun.

Steve, I am enclosing a small check in the amount of $25.00, for your use, which I am sure you can use. If there is anything more I can do, please let me know.

My prayers have been with you since I learned of the incident.

Kindest personal regards.

Sincerely,

As Steve says in his letter, he deserted from an Army base in Germany. He had been based at Fort Rucker, Alabama, when orders for Vietnam came down on him the first time. Those orders were changed. When orders came down for him to go to Germany he was at first relieved, and figured he could make it through. Like many other men still being levied for Vietnam from Germany, Steve was wrong. When the orders came down on him a second time, his decision to desert was crystallized. He is now going to school in Stockholm, and has lived for a time on the Arctic Circle in the north of Sweden.

Steve continues to speak for himself very well. Eighteen

months after his desertion he says: "I accept the desertion and the consequences of it on the basis that there was no other alternative for me. I had to be prepared to accept all consequences because I looked at those consequences as being nowhere near as big a consequence as going to Vietnam. I got myself into a situation where I had to lose. So I accept losing, and in accepting, I lose the opportunity to go back [to the United States], and it is a loss, but it's an accepted one."

chapter 8

"SUCH A GOOD DEAL! (LOCK YOUR DOOR)"

We are all tempted to be Deputies for . . . intellectualized reasons in a time when there are no more observers in the world and we are all Jews.

—Howard Zinn, review of Lewis Feuer's
The Conflict of Generations

Articles like the one in *Look* magazine began to appear with regularity. A particularly good one, from the deserters' point of view, especially in 1968, appeared in *Ebony* magazine. Well written about or not, however, the deserters were news. They were making good copy.

With their increased visibility to the American public, the deserters were faced with a new problem: how to "deal" for an interview with American reporters. The shape of the problem looked like this: members of the American media—newspapermen, radio and television reporters—were hustling their stories. The deserters had a story to tell. That story was going to be told anyway, with or without the cooperation of the deserters. (Stories had been filed about men who had never been interviewed, by reporters who in some cases had not even been to Sweden.) Better, the men reasoned, that their story should be told by them than be reproduced second-hand by the reporters. In other words, the deserters suddenly realized they had a marketable product to sell, their own experience. The result of this discovery was a process known simply as "the deal."

This process was essential to the overall political goal of the deserter community: to get the message back home, especially to those military bases where thousands of their buddies were hungry for a good word. In the wake of the 1968 Tet offensive and the widely publicized fiasco of "Hamburger Hill", GI's were increasingly open to protest and resistance to the war. The deserters saw their own message as food for their fed-up brothers in struggle. Public attention to the deserters' acts of resistance had to help. Deals with the American media people had to be made, even at the cost of some distortion, some outright misrepresentation.

I was to experience many such deals. Indeed, on occasion I pressed journalists to pay the men for interviews. It seemed to me that actual pay, which seldom amounted to more than $20 per interview, increased the self-respect of the individual deserter. The deal also, I think, kept the reporter more honest. If he paid for a story, he was less likely to quote a man out of context.

During the time we were in Stockholm I was involved in more than a hundred such interviews. Relatively few of these necessitated the deal. Most involved putting visitors in touch with various members of the community and letting each side work out an understanding. But some of the arrangements involved a serious judgment about the possible impact of the report at home, the potential for distortion, the likelihood, in a few cases, of the individual reporter being paid by or prepared to work for the United States government. I was particularly skeptical of the bona fides of certain overseas-based American journalists or reporters. Radio Free Europe and the Voice of America spend a lot of the American taxpayer's dollars on just such men.

The fellows had often been burned in similar circumstances, and they wanted to be certain I knew how they felt. Interviews were given by the men, for example, for a story that eventually appeared in the April, 1968, issue of *Pageant* magazine. The story of The Intrepid Four was carried under the title "Young U.S. Sailors Desert to the Russians." The fact that the men had merely gone through the Soviet Union and had been in Sweden since December, 1967, was not even mentioned. Again, *The Atlantic Monthly*, which might be expected to be more sympathetic, carried a story called "We Couldn't Swing With It." The slant in this article was such as to charge the Intrepid Four with dropping out. No mention was made of their own statements. As Des said to me, "The media came and we were like robots. . . . They question, we answer truthfully, and they use us. This time we want revenge," he said, even as he checked *me* out in the process.

None of the arrangements I saw approached, either in ingenuity or sheer crassness, the biggest deal of them all with a man nicknamed, by the deserters involved, "Cash McCall." It is very hard to make this man believable. I can only say that he is a real person; he appeared and spoke as I have recorded it, and the deal was real. The point to underscore is that this is the most outrageous, and hilarious, example of a process that went on all the time, and goes on even now.

On Good Friday morning, April 4, 1969, the first anniversary of the death of Martin Luther King, Jr., a telephone conversation took place in Stockholm. Ron, an American actor, was calling his friend, Des, to say that an American radio broadcaster was in town. "Would you guys be interested in talking with him? It's a straight deal. Down to the bread," said Ron. "Where?" asked Des. "The Grand Hotel," replied Ron. "OK, I'll get some people, but you better guarantee the money," Des warned Ron.

So it was arranged that our visiting American businessman would meet some of his fellow Americans—deserters all from the U.S. armed forces. He represented himself as the owner of a string of radio stations and numerous other ventures. "Cash McCall," so named in parody of an American tycoon in the 1950's, had surfaced in Stockholm. And he wanted an interview—on tape—with the deserters for his radio network. He wanted it very badly.

Des called the Grand Hotel to find Ron. Ron wasn't there but the man himself answered. "Well, I guess we can cut out the middle man," reasoned Des, "and get right down to talking. *What* do you want to do?"

"I just want to set down and talk with you boys," was the answer. "There's not much news about you boys over here. I'd like to do a sort of roundtable discussion thing on tape that I can broadcast over my radio stations." Then he added, "I've got a network of stations, you know, United States and Canada. Yes, sir. I think you'd be interested to know . . ."

Des broke in and said he thought a "trust level" should be established because the guys were a little "touchy." The visitor understood that and asked Des how much food, how much booze, how much money would be needed to reach the "trust level." Money was left open. He wanted to do the tape right away. But our guys had said "nix" to that, so he queried, "Why don't we just get together, have a little party? We can all talk informally and go from there." It was agreed to have the trust level session on Saturday in his room at the Grand Hotel.

The visiting tycoon occupied, it turned out, the biggest suite in the Grand Hotel, "the grandest of Stockholm's grand hotels." The second floor center suite looks out across the waters to the Palace through three bay windows. A large bedroom, two baths, living room with two bars, huge tables and couches and a private study with another bath.

The procession of people to the suite that day must have caused some comment in the hotel lobby. Both straight and hippie types were in attendance. Ron, the actor; the newsman's male assistant; seven American resisters/deserters—Rick of the Intrepid Four; George, from Atlanta; Rob, from Miami; Fred, nicknamed "Cookie"; Richard, a lawyer-deserter from Brooklyn, Fordham, Columbia Law and Fort Knox; Dave, a resister; and Des, the Scottish one. Bruce Bahrenburg of the *Newark Evening News* had come along for an angle on a story of his own. And myself.

Greeting us at the door was the great man himself, in a Western shirt, blue denim jacket and Levi's. Well, not Levi's; maybe blue jeans. You had the feeling he'd never wear that outfit again. But then, you weren't so sure. He was shod with a pair of $100 Western boots, really quite beautiful ones. "All *machismo*," reflected Des later. "He's 100 per cent American male and wants to be sure we know it."

As he offered each of us his business card when we entered, he apologized for doing so. Folks, I don't usually do this in America. I just shake hands and say 'Howdy,' but I'm in Europe so here's my card; remember, I'd just as soon shake your hand." Which he did anyway!

Those present went round the room and introduced themselves. He acknowledged a few and ignored others. It did not seem to make any real difference who was there. This character only needed live bodies in a room to fill the space surrounding him. A blonde Swedish woman in her early thirties attended him, and helped to make us more relaxed. "Well, fellows, this here is Lisa," he introduced her, "and I hope none of you have to ask why she's here. If you don't ask me, I won't have to ask you. OK, fellas?" *What* he didn't have to ask us, or we him, was left unstated. Lisa did not seem embarrassed. She seemed to have a job to do and was doing it efficiently, like a good Swede.

As the drinks were ordered, set up and downed, and as the pit-like bowl of nuts was reduced, our host got to his business. "I came here with an open mind. I just want you boys to teach me. I don't know a thing; in fact, I've made it a point not to read anything. Folks don't know much about you anyway, so go ahead and shoot."

A few guys began to respond on the usual lead—"Why I deserted." But it was clear after a half hour that our interviewer was bored. "Planned concentration," said one fellow later. The guys began to see it as a huge farce—free booze, free food and free "bread." And so the guys began to take him (although really who was taking whom was never resolved). George began rapping about everything and nothing— economic theory, world politics. George was putting him on, he wasn't digging it and George loved it. Others played it straight.

For two hours, this trust level session went on. Apparently, our enterprising American wasn't going to disagree for fear of losing his taping session.

He hadn't taken any chances, either. In the middle of the session, Des looked around the room over the rim of his Scotch and spied a cassette tape recorder hidden in a corner next to one of the bars. The cassette was running. Des ripped off the tape and stuck it in his pocket. He passed it to me, and I held it until Des was ready to confront old Cash McCall with the goods.

"What is this?" asked Des. Old Cash was shocked. "Now, fellows, it wasn't running; you know I wouldn't do that." He was unaccustomed to being confronted. Des shrugged it off and moved to the real issue. "Well, now that we have established a sort of trust level—you are in this for the money, we provide you with the copy. That's business, isn't it? How about our compensation?"

Cash McCall was back again on firm ground. "Well, gentlemen, in addition to being a businessman, I'm also a journalist. I would not want to corrupt my journalism by paying my sources. I do not operate that way. It would not be honest and I'm looking for honesty, fellas." At this, the guys took him straight and figured it had been nice but now we split.

But Ron, the actor and go-between, motioned the journalist to the bedroom. There he pulled off 300 American dollars from a roll of bills and told Ron to get it exchanged to Swedish money. Five minutes later, Ron was back and divvying up 1500 crowns among the deserters in front of everyone. Two hundred crowns ($40) remained and with that the group went out to dinner. But not before they lifted their host's Scotch and rum. The fellows even asked him, "Is it all right if we steal the Scotch? If you say no, we're going to take it anyway." It was all right with Cash; it was just fine.

A hilarious dinner was had by all at the Opera Källaren: nuts, booze; even an enormous Easter egg was in hand. The seven were like boys who had just crashed a neighborhood wedding reception. Afterward, Des remembered trying to give away a bottle of Johnny Walker Black Label to a Swede. The poor man was so scared he ran off, and Des still had his liquid gold.

The day for the taping came. Now it was all business. "Let's see the questions." Old Cash gave them out, the guys looked them over. Some were ruled out, some others included. It was cut and dried. And very dull. A new character appeared on the scene, though. A producer of the Tarzan films and rights owner to Panavision. There was seemingly no end to the parody of American business inherent in the trust level sessions or the taping. As the guys were leaving, Ron, the bag-man, slipped each guy 70 crowns more.

I was not present for the taping session. I asked Richard later about the content of the tape. "We wanted to get one thing straight," he said. "We did not want to rap Sweden. We wanted a decent tape telling something of how it really goes for us. The language training, getting started. Several times we made the analogy that we are immigrants here the way our grandparents and great-grandparents were immigrants to the United States and how much easier it is for us as immigrants to Sweden because of Swedish policy than it was for our grand-parents in America." The guys were making it in Sweden as immigrants and refugees; they were proud of it and wanted the folks at home to know it. That's what was on the tape.

Our American businessman was not impressed with Sweden's policies, however. He got worked up and, for the first time, he lost his cool. "I don't see how you call this a democracy here in Sweden. Why, hell, I used to own a ship," he said. "I owned a radio station in Europe, Radio Nord, and we used to broadcast off that ship." It turned out that his ship was a pirate ship operating in the Stockholm archipelago, and Sweden had to shut it down. The real character of the man showed on his face. He was bitter and enraged. (Des met a Swedish exporter-importer that summer. The Swede said he had sued the broad-caster for using a copyrighted name, Radio Nord, which the Swede himself had copyrighted solely to break the pirate radio business.)

Unwittingly, the man had shown us what he was mostly about: making money. Yet, as far as we have been able to find out, the tape of his interview with the American deserters was never aired. The men have heard no word from him since then. Perhaps he returned and some program director chalked up the episode as one of the boss' weird antics, not knowing *how* weird.

For the men involved, the McCall deal illustrated in a manic way what they were up against in the more routine contacts they had with media representatives. They saw behind the men and women who were sent to interview them a kind of Cash McCall mentality. They saw writers and producers on heavy expense account vacations. And they saw corporate America where money is first and last, and people are only necessary to drive you to the bank.

Walter, another deserter, not involved in this particular adventure, had a way of putting the dictum that guided the men in making the deal. Known as the hustler to end all hustling, Walter could get you to lend him the money to buy a car, and a week later get you to buy it back from him so he could go out and buy another car. Then he would say, charming you with a broad smile, "Such a good deal! Such a good deal!" and add as an aside, "Lock your door."

Before our traveling broadcaster came to Stockholm, the deserters were happy, most of the time, to make whatever deal they could with the journalists. After he had come and gone, they were much tougher at the bargaining table. They had begun to lock their doors behind them.

chapter 9

SOCIOLOGY PLAYS TO MIXED REVIEWS

When we strip away the terminology of the behavioral sciences, we see revealed the mentality of the colonial civil servant, persuaded of the benevolence of the mother country and the correctness of its vision of world order, and convinced that he understands the true interests of the backward peoples whose welfare he is to administer.

—Noam Chomsky, *American Power and the New Mandarins*

Efforts at interpreting the deserter community, some by the men themselves and some by outsiders, seemed never-ending. The Army had its own point of view. We have seen a sample of civilian reaction in the correspondence between Steve and his employer. The story of a particularly outrageous character has illustrated the general encounter with newsmen. Strangely, the social scientists proved to be an even more varied group.

Soon after our arrival in Stockholm, I received a letter from an American sociologist on the faculty of a prominent university in the northeastern part of the country. The writer—we shall call him Doctor R.—an Associate Professor of Sociology, explained that he was about to come to Stockholm "to interview military deserters" over a two-month period that summer. Doctor R. asked for my help. He remarked that the major problem he expected to encounter was "obtaining sponsorship from the organizations which represent these young men," so that he could "get in touch with a fairly large number of individuals."

"The Deserter as a Political Deviant"

Doctor R. was quite open and enclosed his project proposal in his letter.

Title of Project: The Deserter as a Political Deviant.

The goal of this study will be to assess theories of deviant behavior in light of case material in the neglected area of political deviance. Merton and others have recognized this gap, and recent developments make it possible to remedy this deficiency. As a result of polarization over the war, the incidence of political offenses has risen sharply. Deserters who have obtained political asylum in Sweden constitute *an important category of offenders*. [Author's italics] Unlike draft resisters in Canada, they are military personnel living as civilians in a linguistically alien environment far from home. *Their predicament is of strategic importance for the study of deviance*. [Author's italics] It is anticipated that concepts such as latency, contingency factors in certification, and socialization in deviant norms will prove inapplicable. Such findings would lead to the correction of current theories based on studies of other kinds of deviance.

After referring to a "sample" of thirty to forty "field interviews" and his ability to speak Swedish (he had been a student at the University of Stockholm), Doctor R. continued his proposal with a list of the tools he would use in his study.

Components of the study will include the following: *a*) data on SES levels, regional background, developmental history, educational level, and occupational goals; *b*) steps in the decision-making process, motives for desertion, precipitating events, interpersonal and group influences; *c*) adjustment to deviant status, identity problems, future plans (permanent exile, surrender to authorities, hopes for amnesty or change in criteria for C.O. [conscientious objector] status, etc.) and sources of group support, including communication with friends and relatives. If possible, a follow-up on some of these persons in the U.S. will be attempted at a later date.

For this study Doctor R. had received a faculty research fellowship in the amount of $2,575, which was noted on the project proposal. The professor earned his Ph.D. from New York University and had been an analyst in social science for the National Institutes of Mental Health. His academic qualifications appeared to be bona fide. He had been licensed by his profession to practice within it, and he was going about just that.

The trouble lay in that fact. Within the profession of sociology there is a category of study called "social deviance." Examples of behavior studied in this manner might include a group of drug addicts, persons convicted of white-collar crime or sharecroppers transplanted from the farm to a city. From the point of view of the social scientist the study of such groups of people is "objective," that is, neither a moral nor a political judgment may be formed about the *merit* of the behavior in question. Thus Doctor R. saw his project with the deserters as having "strategic importance for the study of deviance."

This particular approach may work well if the people under study accept the view of the outside observer that they are indeed deviants from the norms of society. A group of convicts might agree, for example, to discuss their past histories and motivations that led them into criminal behavior. When the people under proposed study, however, reject the description of themselves as "deviants," as almost any politically or socially dissident group might, the social scientist has a problem. The interests of the individuals in the group and the social scientist are in conflict. The primary fear of the dissidents is that the material garnered by the scientist becomes a weapon in the hands of an Establishment potentially able to oppress the group even further.

Doctor R. was vaguely aware that there might be some tension between him and his subjects. "Although the tone of the project summary is coldly analytical," he wrote to me, "I want very much to be able to communicate some of the 'findings' on a more experiential level. For this purpose sound tapes would be of great value, if some of the men are willing to permit taped interviews." Even this limited awareness, however, widened the distance between himself and the exile community. The purpose of getting taped interviews, he said, was *for him* to "communicate some of [his] findings."

I advised Doctor R. by mail that the deserter-resister community had been badly exploited by reporters and researchers. Because of their fears, I warned him, he could expect little cooperation from me. I indicated that the men—and women as well, for Doctor R. wished to meet them—did not see themselves as "deviants." As Don E. from Guilford, Connecticut expressed it, "Sure, we go along with him, and out of the 'research' comes another 'Deserter as Political Pervert' article." Doctor R. later told me that he had gotten this message from my letter but he believed that he could win both me and the men over.

The Arrival of Doctor R.

When he did arrive in Stockholm in early July, we were prepared for him. Copies of the proposal had been circulated, and people rather looked forward to finding out who this character was. It turned out that he had assumed all along that we, the Clergy and Laymen Sweden Project people, would be interested in helping him out. When I told him in person that we could not, and gave my reasons, he was genuinely shocked. He was counting on us.

Since his own motives were sincere, he could not seem to comprehend that his project could be injurious to the interests of the community in any way. He further believed that "the church," in so far as we were church-and-synagogue connected, would approve of his efforts and bless them with our own cooperation. I was to discover an important lesson from our dealings with this man: when a representative of the academic community assumes the cooperation of the church in the study of oppressed groups in our society, a great deal is revealed about both institutions. Both the academy and the church have to change their stance substantially in regard to those considered by the society to be deviants. In our situation, our quarrel was not with Doctor R. but with the model of study he embodied. Committed as he was, and is, to a concept of "objective scholarship," he rendered himself incapable of understanding the people he sought to study. Actual truth-seeking, it seems to me, is precisely subversive of such goals and methods as Doctor R., and social science generally, employ when dealing with oppressed groups who are fighting for their lives and destinies.

(Two Roman Catholic sociologists were to visit while we were there and took views rather different from Doctor R.'s. Dr. Gordon Zahn, of Boston University, author of *German Catholics and Hitler's Wars* and *In Solitary Witness*, the life of Franz Jägerstätter, martyred in World War II for conscientiously refusing military service in Hitler's army, came among us. He, too, hoped that sometime a serious sociological study could be done *with* the deserters. That was the difference—*with* them. Dr. Zahn recognizes "conscientious desertion," as he puts it, and believes that the men themselves can best interpret their own actions and motivations. Msgr. Paul Hanley Furfey, a giant and veteran among Catholic social scientists, author of *Fire on Earth* and *The Respectable Murders: Social Evil and Christian Conscience*, visited with us in August. He was more skeptical of the prospect of social research among the men.)

After being blocked by me, and then by the American Deserters Committee, Doctor R. visited around the edges of the community. He managed a trip to Uppsala, a visit with Dr. Robert Rommel, an American psychologist who had engaged some of the deserters in sensitivity training, and some isolated sessions with a handful of the deserters. He was in great danger of losing his entire project, he told us. He begged for our help. "The man has to be straight," one fellow remarked, " 'cause no one else could come on like that and expect us to buy in." Collectively, the American Deserters Committee had put out the word that they had changed their group mind and decided to see Doctor R. By now a number of persons had copies of the proposal that Doctor R. had sent, and they were curious.

Nearly six weeks had passed since Doctor R.'s arrival. He

had made contact with a Swedish teacher named "Finn." At the sociologist's request, Finn arranged a meeting with what was supposed to be a group of a half-dozen people. It happened that one of the deserters involved at this stage was also involved with the American Deserters Committee. So when Doctor R. arrived for his small-group discussion he found instead a much larger meeting of twenty-five people gathered to interview him. Several of the people whom the Doctor had seen in Uppsala came to Stockholm seriously to discuss the nature of the professor's project. And they were interested in asking him some questions.

The evening turned out to be an encounter with Doctor R., not with the deserters. It was courteously but determinedly conducted. That is, there was no letting up in the examination of the visitor. Someone pointed out that even the deserters' refusal to answer the Doctor's questions or to participate in his project would be grist for his mill, and so people had to be aware of being "interviewed" although they intended otherwise. Doctor R. seemed to most of the persons I talked with afterward to be disturbed by this latest and, as it turned out, last failure to get his field interviews. People felt he had been gracious enough about accepting their rebuffs, but that he did not comprehend what their resistance was all about. After six weeks, he still seemed to see it somehow as a failure in his own approach and not inherent in his original thesis. He left Stockholm shortly after that meeting.

Report to the Academy

One April morning in the spring after our return, I received a telephone call from a New York friend who had heard me refer to the doctor and his research project. Jay Schulman, a sociologist at City College of New York, advised me that on a coming Saturday morning (April 18, 1970) Doctor R. was to deliver a paper before a group of his colleagues in the Eastern Sociological Society's Annual Meeting at the New York Hilton

Hotel. The paper was listed and entitled "Encounter with Deserters." "Tom, I thought you'd like to know," said Jay.

The paper was presented, along with two others on alcoholics and on criminals or law-breakers, under the sectional theme of "Deviance." Actually, Doctor R. chose to comment on his study rather than read his paper. He said he had gone to encounter the deserters and encountered himself instead; that he had given up any further thought of dealing with the deserter question in terms of political deviance and that he refused to believe that the American Deserters Committee could be considered representative of the feelings of other deserters in Sweden, and in Canada where he had also gone. He concluded, however, "This is not a terminal project. This paper was turned down by ten journals, accepted for hearing by two professional associations, and I have signed a contract to do a book. I believe in 'openness.' If I come to the point where I believe that I should take up a gun, I will do that. Until then I go on."

Dr. Edward Sagarin, Professor of Criminology at New York University, was the discussant for the three papers. After making his critique of the other papers, Doctor Sagarin proceeded to Doctor R.'s paper. He felt strongly disposed against it, he said. Sagarin pointed out the paper had not been read to the assembled body, and that if it had, people would understand why it had been turned down by the ten professional journals. In Sagarin's words, "It is a piece of junk." He called Doctor R.'s paper "a wail of woe, a journalistic peregrination and pilgrimage of a person going around from one place to another." He added that the difference between journalists and sociologists is that journalists can write. He closed with the remark, "If I had been screwed by as many people as this man claims to have been, I would have to consider that I may be a whore." Doctor R. had been put down by a professional and a colleague; in manner it was like surgery. I felt compassion and wondered if the patient would live.

In one sense, Professor Sagarin was cruel. Doctor R. made

quite a point of having discovered something about himself. In his "post mortem" (sic) Doctor R. wrote:

In terms of its original objectives, this study was a signal failure. When it became clear that a conventional approach was out of the question, the original plan was modified. Nevertheless, resistance hardened to such a point that even the uncommitted deserters fell into line with the ADC. In this respect, the author's presence helped to solidify the deserter community. The community defined the situation as a zero-sum game in which any gain for the investigator meant a loss for all other players. He was a representative of the academic establishment, and his findings would fall into the hands of the enemies of the community. Although he might be personally sympathetic, his motives were perceived as shallow, since he was not active in any radical organization, had sacrificed nothing in coming to Sweden, and could only gain in terms of his career. Finally, the relatively privileged position to which he would return after completing his hit-and-run study was a source of resentment to persons facing a very uncertain future. In the eyes of the deserters, it was the sociologist who was the deviant. Thus, the encounter with deserters became an encounter with self, and the effect on the investigator was as unsettling as the portrait of Dorian Gray.

[To this point Professor Sagarin remarked that "R. doesn't need a portrait of Dorian Gray; when he looks in the mirror he can see himself."]

The familiar self is that of a certified professional whose projects have been given the stamp of approval by his respected peers. His passport is the search for truth, and although it is supposed to be valid anywhere he is generously prepared to accept a "refusal rate" of, say, 10 per cent. Therefore, it is astonishing when the passport is returned with a question: "Whose truth? And for whom?" Suddenly the sociologist finds himself surrounded in his own preserve. The sociology of knowledge is his domain. What are his "subjects" doing here? . . .

Deserters are the boy [sic] next door; your neighbor's son, my neighbor's brother. He is safe in Sweden, but he is not there on a lark. Tourists and sociologists are his enemies, because they remind him of home. Of course, he is homesick but we must understand the double meaning of that term. The Senate's fist-shaking will not bring him back, nor will the liberal's appeal for presidential amnesty.

If America wants her sons back it will have to stop behaving like a prodigal father, or it will lose even the children who are still at home.

What is happening is that the docile populations which we found convenient for research purposes are transforming themselves into communities. They are profoundly conscious, and they are organized. They have veto power, and we can only hope that they have creative potential as well. Perhaps they entertain the same hopes for us.

This quotation is made at some length to show that Doctor R. had made considerable progress in understanding what he was about. If he had left the matter somewhere along the line of the conclusion to his paper, his change would be convincing. During the discussion that followed the presentation of the paper, however, I put a question to him and he could not answer it to my satisfaction. In the question-and-answer period he had stated that he was going on with his research and that it was not terminal. I asked *why*, if he had been so consistently rebuffed in his research, it was *not* terminal. At first he did not answer. When it was put to him again by another questioner, he pleaded "openness," and would not, or could not, develop his point any further. It seemed to me that Doctor R. had not gotten the message, after all.

Thus, there is a contradiction between Doctor R.'s personal growth and the sustaining assumptions that guide him professionally. I believe that this same contradiction exists in many professional people within our society, and that an increasing number of them recognize it. Take as an example the subsection, "deviance," in the discipline of sociology. Deviance is defined by those who set the norms that have allegedly been broken. No amount of personal growth by an individual observer is permitted to challenge this basic assumption. The very existence and pursuit of such studies as "deviance" reveal a value-orientation about the disciplines *regardless* of the sympathies of the researcher involved. When a researcher imagines that his study is objective in its search for truth, he fails to understand the complicity of his discipline in the established order and the inherent predisposition of his conclusions to be politically useful to those who seek to control the very behavior he is studying.

Social research among oppressed peoples is further complicated by a factor rather beyond the accounting here. "Political deviants," again to use the terminology of the discipline of sociology, generally see themselves as acting with a sense of moral and social rightness. To ignore this variable is to render any study in this area meaningless. Precisely because of this, *the deserters can be represented only by themselves*, not by any sociologist, not by this writer, not by any outside organization or interest, however sympathetic.

"An important category of offenders," from another point of view, for example, might well be in the White House, in the Pentagon, in the Congress of the United States and in the war-related defense industries. Carl A. Gerstacker, Chairman of the Board of Dow Chemical Company, has often remarked, about his corporation's production of napalm and herbicides for use in Vietnam, that it was not his or his company's province to make a moral or political judgment about the policies of the government. As long as the government needed their assistance, Dow would comply. Yet it was argued at Nuremberg that reasonable men must deviate from policies they discover to contravene international law and agreement and which they believe to be criminal, in fact or by intent. For "while some are guilty, all are responsible," Mr. Gerstacker and Dow power notwithstanding.

A radically new deviance amounting to awakening from a nightmare is necessary if America is to endure its dark night of the soul and mankind to survive as a working member of the earth household. A revolutionary struggle is *normative* for man; the rest is corruption or distortion.

This offending view of the world is well caught in lines from a song by the folk-rock group, "Creedence Clearwater Revival":

> Saw the people standing
> Thousand years in chains

Somebody says it's different now
Look, it's just the same

Pharaohs spin the message
Round and round the truth

They could've saved a million people
How can I tell you?*

The problem with the Doctor R.'s of the world is that with the best of intentions they are working for the Pharaohs while there is a new Exodus afoot, and they do not even know where they stand. Perhaps the waters of a new creation will swallow them up as the horse's rider was thrown to the sea in the Exodus out of Egypt. It is certain that if their heads are not cleared, if they know not which way they are going, they will never make it into the Promised Land.

An Observer Participates

People can change their whole outlook, however, and some do. Dan P. is an example. In August, 1968, Dan came to Stockholm, visited with members of the American Deserters Committee and others, and made plans to return a year later to do his Ph.D. thesis on the deserters. Dan is black, and he is a sociologist. Currently he is associate dean of the College of Humanities at Stanford University. He was well received his first time around and there was no reason for him to think that his plan of study would not go well. Further, he knew the importance of relating to the men not as objects, but as subjects, as persons who could not and would not be used against their will. So Dan set himself up in Uppsala in the fall of 1969 and began to work closely with the men there. By this time, there were some twenty fellows who had either found jobs or entered the University of Uppsala. A smaller group would lend itself to closer personal knowledge of the actual situation facing the men and how they related to it.

* Reprinted by permission of Jondora Music.

What happened to Dan is a reminder of many good things in life. He became well liked. He got to know the men. He "rapped" with them hours on end. He became involved in their struggle with Swedish social authorities. He became involved in their own attempt at internal organization through the evolution of the American Deserters Committee at Uppsala. He seemed to have no ulterior motive, although the deserters were quite aware of his intended research. Yet when he asked outright for permission to have personal interviews to go into their backgrounds, attitudes toward parents, trouble with the law, schooling and the like, they balked. Beyond the level of trust he had built up with them and they with him, they could not go. Further, Dan found himself at odds with Jerry, the chairman of the ADC there. So involved was Dan that he began to suspect that Jerry might be an agent, because certain of Jerry's positions and actions had seemed to be self-defeating. Jerry, in turn, had done some checking on Dan, with a similar charge in mind.

Dan was clearly no longer a "participant observer," as he hoped to be and as was his role-model for researching the scene. Dan gave up all thought of doing his thesis on the men; he limited himself to an article he "might publish some time." Finally, Dan had to leave Uppsala for Stockholm for rest and rehabilitation. The internal struggle became too much for him to cope with and, to his credit, he knew it. The pain within him was great. The situation had "blown his mind," and he needed to talk it out. In late December he rejoined his wife who had been studying in England, and returned to the States. He found some good friends, but he had lost his thesis. Without intending it, I am sure, the men had so affected him that he could no longer see them in the same light as he had before. His "laboratory" had blown up and he didn't seem to mind. By now it may all seem unreal to him, so far is he removed from what they went through together. But it was quite real and, more important, he was quite real to us at the time.

I remember a lovely poem, "Who Has Seen the Wind?"

which warns of a hazard any one of us faces when, like Dan, we get overinvolved. It is by Robert Kaufman, a young American poet.

> A Spanish sculptor named Cherino
> Has seen the wind.
> He says it is shaped like a coil of hardened copper
> And spirals into itself and out again,
> That it is very heavy
> And can break your toe if it falls on your foot.
>
> Be careful when you are moving the wind;
> It can put you in the hospital

Working Socially

Someone else who tried "moving the wind" with us is Mrs. Beatrice Seitzman, an associate professor of Social Work in Columbia University's School of Social Work. Mrs. Seitzman, a slightly greying woman in her early forties, was seized in the early spring by an impulse to give her summer over to something useful for others. She announced one day to friends that "I'm going to Stockholm to work with the deserters and that guy, Hayes." She could scarcely believe it herself, it was so presumptuous. After she did some checking on us, and we on her, we made plans for her to spend July and August with us in Stockholm. She was no sooner in town than we had her set up in an apartment (which she often had to share with new deserters coming in) and into a session in which the famous Doctor R. briefed us on his intentions. Mrs. Seitzman made herself invaluable to us and to Mrs. Nystrom. Probably no one but she could have fitted in so well or done so much in the time she was there. I felt within a week that her coming was divinely inspired. The world should be seized by the dream or impulse that overtook this woman.

Mrs. Seitzman said on her return to the States in late August;

"I feel like the American journalist who spent a month in Russia in the early period of the Revolution and with indecent haste rushed into publication with authoritative writings on the world's first experiment with socialism.

"The deserter scene is such a complex interrelation of social, political and human themes in constant interaction with larger world conflict that I need to disclaim the role of expert. I am a social worker with strong convictions and compassion for people struggling for freedom. This led me into participating in the lives of a small group of deserters for a brief eight-week period.

"The overriding feeling that accompanied my work this summer, one that I fully expect will never leave me, is that of an acceleration of anger against our government. The anger has always been there against the fruitless, murderous war in Vietnam. This war has not only taken the lives of the Vietnamese and Americans but is also responsible for depriving these 400 men of the basic human option of where to live out one's life. At a time when a young man should be planning how to live his life in an environment receptive to his aspirations, the deserter must search for housing and struggle with the difficult Swedish language so that he can find work or study in the university. An alien in a world he never made, he is lonely for family and friends and the familiar signposts of his own culture.

"Yet the deserters do not come off an angry young men. The subjective reactions to finding themselves in diaspora are hidden. There is little time for the emotional expenditure that may drain off the energy required to make it in this foreign land. Because they do not see the possibility of amnesty, it is not talked about. They are heavily involved in settling in because this is where they expect to spend the rest of their lives. But there is little doubt that many of the underlying themes reveal a kind of longing for their homeland mixed with marked determination to close off remembrance with the country that in fact caused their decision to desert.

"I am reminded of Pat, a tall, attractive student at the University of Uppsala. He is an extremely warm young man whose wife, Linda, and child, Shawn, live in a lovely student dorm. I asked Pat, as I asked so many of the other deserters, if there was anything I could do for him when I returned. His eyes brimmed with tears; suddenly looking like a helpless child, he said in the saddest tones I have ever heard, 'I want to see my mother.'

"To live and work in Stockholm is to find oneself in a sense in the midst of a battleground where the human drama is recounted and reacted every day. The stories of the journey into exile stagger the imagination. One of the fairly recent arrivals, the son of a retired Marine officer, jumped ship in Australia. With the help of an Australian family, he stowed away in another ship for forty-five days and made his way to Sweden via the Orient. Then, there is Michael who received his order for Vietnam while on the West Coast. He then went to a Scandinavian Airways reservation desk dressed in Army attire requesting one-way passage to Scandinavia. He did not realize that he might have selected a less obtrusive garb or approach for leaving the U.S. But he got there.

"The intensity of the living situation in Sweden is equally staggering. One unforgettable scene took place the night before I left, at a house in Stockholm. It is the night headquarters of the American Deserters Committee (ADC) and houses at least ten deserters. The doorbell rang; in walked two of the straightest guys I have ever seen, with short hair, dark suits and ties. They were the most frightened young men I have ever seen, and had just arrived from an Army base in Germany. Within a few moments, a small group of veteran deserters (anyone who is there more than a month is practically a veteran) spontaneously gathered around them. It was one of the most supportive human exchanges that I have ever seen in the "people enterprise." Soon phone calls were underway and overnight housing was arranged though never consummated since both guys fell asleep while talking. They spent the night on the living room couch, well nurtured and cared for by their compatriots in exile.

"Because housing is very scarce, much of my experience this summer is associated with the picture of the deserter always with suitcase or knapsack in hand. It is a rare deserter and his family who can claim an apartment that is really their own. My daughter encapsulated the housing situation quite well when she wrote me this summer. She was convinced that I was the only mother in the whole world who was running a crash pad for deserters.

"While many young men decide to desert rather than ship out to Vietnam, I was impressed by the large number whose desertion was in response to life in the armed forces. Many enlisted young men and even some draftees had expected that the Army would provide them with some kind of work training or educational opportunities that had not been available to them as civilians. Instead they found themselves unable to comply with the demands of an authoritarian and dehumanizing military system with no opportunity for change or dissent. They then made the decision to desert.

"Every possible shade of political opinion is represented in the deserter community. There are those who disclaim the political implications of the act of desertion. Then, there are those who see desertion as an act of conscience against an imperialist power. Some see desertion as part of an international movement against the United States. At no point, however, did I talk to any deserter who was not capable of moving from the subjective reasons for desertion into making some of the basic connections with his country's foreign policy. It is indeed ironic that the authoritarian Army system has inadvertently politicized these young men and provided a learning experience on the nature of political and social systems that would never have been available in the classroom."

As Mrs. Seitzman makes clear, there is no way to encounter the deserters without encountering oneself. It was this fact that she, Dan P. and Doctor R. found out in turn. Mrs. Seitzman became most deeply involved personally when two of our men died within eight days of each other and less then two weeks after her arrival. Bob Sylvia was on the island of Gotland, off the Swedish east coast, when he committed suicide by asphyxiation while very depressed. Mrs. Seitzman happened to be on the island that weekend and talked with the young Swedish FNL-ers (National Front for Liberation of Sweden) who knew Bob. On July 10, Greg Vitarelle of Amarillo, Texas, died in a drowning accident in front of the Palace in Stockholm. Mrs. Seitzman was there to help Greg's friends, his fiancée, Nita Molander, and the rest of us to work through our grief and make arrangements for returning Greg's body. After such experiences one no longer imagines himself a neutral observer. One thing about "Bea," as we know her, became clear to us: her humanity informs and controls her profession. It is never the other way around.

"I'll Never Get Another Grant . . ."

Writing in the *New York Review of Books,** Paul Goodman asks, "Can Technology Be Humane?" He says of the social sciences and their supposed neutrality:

The state of the behavioral sciences is, if anything, even worse [than the physical sciences]. Their claim to moral and political neutrality becomes, in effect, a means of diverting atention from glaring social evils, and they are in fact used—or would be if they worked—for warfare and social engineering, manipulation of people for the political and economic purposes of the powers that be. This is an especially sad betrayal since, in the not-too-distant past, the objective social sciences were developed lately to dissolve orthodoxy, irrational authority, and taboo. They were heretical and intellectually revolutionary, as the physical sciences had been in their own Heroic Age, and they weren't getting grants.

To make the point irrefutable, I think, on three different occasions Doctor R. said to the deserters or to me, "Look, if I

* November 20, 1969, p. 27.

don't get your cooperation, I'll never get another grant." We were incredulous, but that did not change the fact that this American social scientist believed he could ask for, and receive, help on that basis. This is a grim indictment, indeed. Fortunately for us in Stockholm, social scientists are a mixed bag. Overall, we were dealt with well.

chapter 10

EASY RIDIN' AMERIKA

BILLY: All we represent to them, man, is somebody needs a haircut.

GEORGE: What you represent to them is freedom.

. . . .

I mean, it's real hard to be free when you are bought and sold in the marketplace. 'Course don't even tell anybody that they're not free, cause then they're gonna get real busy killin' and maimin' to prove to you that they are. Oh, yeah—they're gonna talk to you, and talk to you, and talk to you about individual freedom but they see a free individual, it's gonna scare 'em.

BILLY: Well, that don't make 'em runnin' scared.

GEORGE: No. It makes 'em dangerous.

> —Peter Fonda, Dennis Hopper and Terry Southern, screenplay for *Easy Rider**

The Peter Fonda–Dennis Hopper–Terry Southern film, *Easy Rider*, came through Stockholm in early July, 1969. This was the time of the annual July Fourth doings at the American Embassy. Each year the Embassy in Stockholm issues a general invitation for all Americans and their friends to celebrate the festival of American independence on its lawn. (Why not, some day, a festival of world interdependence?) The year 1969 was

---

* From *Easy Rider* by Peter Fonda, Dennis Hopper and Terry Southern. Copyright © 1969 by Raybert Productions, Inc. Reprinted by arrangement with The New American Library, Inc., New York.

no exception, in spite of the absence of any ambassador. (The Johnson administration appointee, William Heath, was withdrawn in January, 1969.) Turner Cameron, deputy chief of mission, was host.

And that afternoon, almost according to a movement script, the American Deserters Committee "brought the war home" to the Embassy.

Cooperating in the event was the Swedish-American Society of Stockholm. A party was held on the grounds in front of "the Glass Menagerie," as the Embassy is called by friend and foe. Among friends it was to be a Fourth as usual: hot dogs, soda, pony rides and games for the kiddies, lots of all-American friendliness and fun. Among the sponsors who funded the occasion were the Ford Motor Company, General Motors, Coca-Cola, Goodyear, IBM Svenska AB, the 3M Company, Pan American Airways, Esso and the two major Swedish banks, Svenska Handelsbanken and the Wallenbergs' Enskilda Banken. Probably the sponsors considered their participation an entirely appropriate investment, good for business and *very* good for deteriorating Swedish-American relations. That there was a terrible anachronism, not to say affront, in such a celebration in any American Embassy in the midst of the ongoing war in Vietnam did not seem to occur to anyone.

Except the deserters and *their* friends. Thirty-five members of the American Deserters Committee brought the war home to the United States government outpost in Stockholm. The men tried to show the complicity of Swedish and American businessmen in just such "good clean fun." When a paid orchestra began to play the national anthems of both countries, several of the deserters sat down in front of the crowd while the remainder stood with clenched fists raised. It was the "all power to the people" salute, as the Committee stated, "to show solidarity with the exploited masses now rising against U.S. imperialism around the world." Someone from the Embassy announced that the demonstrators were disturbing a "diplomatic meeting" and therefore should be removed. The men—

and women, for there were wives, friends and co-workers among them—answered, "We are not leaving until the U.S. gets out of Vietnam." As quickly as a good phrase becomes a slogan, plain clothed U.S. Marines, the deserters' former compatriots, grabbed each one and handed him or her over to Stockholm police. Eight people were arrested, Michelle Huth was beaten and the demonstration became an all-American picnic again. When I talked with several of the people later they remarked that they could not see "independence" as a slogan for 1776 but only as a living principle, "the right of the Vietnamese people and all peoples around the world."

Captain America Visits Stockholm

So the stage was set for the coming into town of the film, *Easy Rider*. The framework of that film is now familiar to many. The two main characters, Wyatt and Billy, are young anti-heroes who, as the film opens, are paid off for their part in a cocaine deal on the Mexican border. With their tainted "bread" in one motorbike's gas tank, they head for a cross-country ride along high desert roads to New Orleans and the Mardi Gras celebration. Billy wears his Kit Carson jacket and a bush hat while Wyatt is "Captain America" in a black leather jacket with a mini-flag sewn on the back. Because they look like the outcasts they turn out to be, they must camp by the road. There is no room for them in a society of motels. In the course of the journey they meet a number of odd sorts, notably a Southern ACLU-type lawyer, George Hanson, whom they encounter in a jail where Hanson was locked up for drunkenness. The discovery of themselves, especially Wyatt's reflection, revolves around their making it from their original immoral act (selling cocaine in the first place) to a dead end. Wyatt seems to understand their self-contradiction when he tells Billy on the road beyond New Orleans, "We blew it."

Dennis Hopper, who plays Billy, has said instructively:*

* From an interview published by Underground Press Service.

I know when we were making the movie, we could feel this: the whole country seemed to be burning up—Negroes, hippies, students. The country was on fire. And I meant to work this feeling into the symbols in the movie: like Peter's [Fonda] bike, Captain America's Great Chrome Bike—that beautiful machine covered with stars and stripes is America. I'm not sure that people understood, but that bike with all the money in the gas tank is America and we've got all our money in a gas tank—and that any moment we can be shot off it—BOOM—explosion—that's the end: we go up in flames.

Hopper is concerned about a misreading that many made of the cocaine deal, seeing a glorification of it, rather than an exposure of its meaning.

At the start of the movie, Peter and I do a very American thing— we commit a crime, we go for the easy money. We go for the easy money and we're free. That's one of the big problems with the country right now: everybody's going for the easy money. I think Americans basically feel the criminal way is all right *if you don't get caught*: crime pays, *if* you get away with it . . . "We blew it" means to me that they could have spent that energy in something other than smuggling cocaine, could have done something other than help the society destroy itself.

Swedish film reviewers raved. They abstracted from it, however, the theme of the violence in American life. Clues were drawn from it to search out the meaning of the 1968 Chicago Convention, racism in America and our political assassinations. Thus on the evening of the Fourth of July many of us were in the cinema on Birger Jarlsgatan in Stockholm. Among us was a newly arrived delegation of twenty-five American high school students on a Friends World College (Long Island, New York) tour. Bert and Honey Knopp of Westport, Connecticut, old friends through their work with the American Friends Service Committee, were the tour guides. Linda Meyers, then a staff worker for People for Human Rights in Philadelphia, was on board. And many of the deserters and resisters. In all there were perhaps seventy-five Americans in the theater that night.

I remember a good deal about that evening and the discussions that followed. Seeing the film on the night of the Fourth seemed a most appropriate remembrance of the origins of our republic. Many others saw it in the weeks thereafter. Afterward, folks would come around to our apartment to talk out the movie's meaning for them. The deserters and resisters, and their wives and girls, were all moved quite deeply by the film. While it meant something different to everyone, it seemed to mean *something* to everyone. I had never known a film to have such an effect upon a group of people whom I knew well.

"You know, this country used to be . . ."

How was it that so many different people in this group of exiles could identify with this film? See yourself as Captain America? Not so much, I thought. Clearly, *Easy Rider* is a kind of contemporary Clifford Odets–message film. But what was the message these people were hearing? Two fellows told me they had been through just those parts of the South and Southwest, one on a Harley himself. One told me that he thought he recognized his own hometown. Quite a few identified with the townspeople, with minor characters at the commune, and perhaps this reflects their origins in working-class, often rural, America.

The substance of the film story is by no means as fictional as most Americans might think. I was viewing some film clips of the men in Canada for a producer and crew who were doing a special for a Rochester, New York, television station. One segment of their film had two fellows, one black and one white, whose car had blown up (on its own) at seven o'clock on a Saturday morning in Westminster, Arkansas. When they went for help, the local Klan was notified that hippies were in the area. They began their escape. Before they could get away they were "busted" for blocking traffic. They counted themselves quite lucky, however, for both of them were deserters living underground at that time, and their identity went undiscovered. As they told their story on film there was little embellishment, and no humor.

Still, most of the fellows in Sweden admitted that they had not experienced anything like the film's substantive content. Yet they reasoned, "If you want to know why I split, see that film." Another quipped, "See America first! See *Easy Rider!*"

Many volunteered that the film's theme stuck to the lips of the Southern lawyer, George Hanson (played by Jack Nicholson): "You know, this country used to be a helluva nice place to live in. I can't understand what's gone wrong with it." The phrase became a motto for a while and was shortened to "You know, this country . . ." and was followed by a warm and knowing chuckle. Something in this phrase spoke to the deserters' condition. It was one more piece in the sorting out of a puzzle, the game they play seriously and excel in. You might have thought from some of their comments that Fonda and Hopper were actually AWOL's in disguise, surfacing out of the American underground where many of the men had roamed before seeking permanent resettlement.

For myself, I remember thinking that *Easy Rider* was like a successful surgery performed on Western culture. But the patient had died. In this light the venom in the picture seems only partly therapeutic. The rest is sick, very sick. Transparently, the film is not about the South, a fact that was recognized by almost everyone. An exception was a young man unrelated to the deserters-resisters but who saw himself as an émigré. At a taping of a segment on exile for NBC's program, "First Tuesday," he remarked that what really frightened him about the movie was that "something like that could happen in the United States." His fellow Americans present jumped on him to ask where he had been during the 1960's.

Mike Castle, a folk and blues singer and a deserter, came up with one of the best comments. "Most folks [at home]," he said, "will think of the South when they see it. And the point is that it's not even about the U.S. It's about the collapse of Western values around the violence of its foundations." That even one among the men should articulate this insight gives the reader some idea where the others are in their thinking generally. The war, the system and their action in response "transnationalizes" them. They seek a cleaner flag, or no flag at all.

A Generation Bridge

Chuck's parents came over from Charlestown, West Virginia, to see their son about that time. Chuck had been a West Point appointee and had refused the appointment to take a science scholarship elsewhere. Drafted, Chuck had split from what he considered the insanity of the military system. He discovered within himself a profound abhorrence to war and war-making, and his objection was ignored by the military. Chuck could not ignore it. His parents were seeing him for the first time since he had deserted in 1968. Their son, and his American fiancée, Rosemary (they are now married and living in Stockholm), took the parents to see the film.

The parents were visibly upset by *Easy Rider*. They were disturbed that anyone should think that "*that* is a picture of the 'real' America." They felt deeply it is this kind of movie that creates and perpetuates the problems in America. The discussions between the two couples were lively indeed. Said the parents, "Foreigners get a wrong idea about us and then the kooks at home just pick up on it. America just isn't like that and it's wrong to show a movie like that."

Regardless of whether *Easy Rider* is a literal rendition of experience in America (the parents obviously felt it was not), the film does have a crossgenerational significance. Chuck and Rosemary spent a good deal of time, for example, trying to interpret the film to their folks. Chuck spoke of the paralyzing fear he saw in the movie being much like the fear induced by military indoctrination. The Southerners' fear of strangers was like the drill sergeant's fear of "gooks" and "kooks." Chuck and Rosemary also saw in the film a fear of *self*-discovery, not only of strangers, a character flaw he finds in his fellow Americans as well as in himself.

What struck me about this crossgenerational encounter was how astonishingly effective a means of communication the film had been for them. It may have been the first realization on his parents' part of how deep was Chuck's conviction as to the rightness of his desertion from the Army and "all the rest." It may also have been helpful for the younger couple to find some things they could talk about, some things that all four felt were important enough to get worked up about. If *Easy Rider* is "badly organized rage," as one critic has complained, the fact that the rage within the American spirit was organized at all is surely in the film's favor.

Finding Solid Ground

Something else in the film affected the community. It was identified but not quite articulated. This feeling was caught in a phrase quipped by a deserter in another context: "The Deserter as Paranoid." There was a fascination with the fears of Captain America and his buddy that I could not have predicted. Several folks noted that they found themselves looking "over their shoulders" again after having thought they had thrown such fears aside. A man who has deserted the U.S. armed forces still sees himself as a hunted man. So the murder-by-night scene in the movie had far more impact on us there than the long "tripping" in New Orleans.

It is hard to communicate such a view of America, or of oneself, unless you yourself have "looked over your own shoulder." "Don't look back" is an injunction not easily followed if you were beaten in Chicago or spent time in the Presidio stockade. My first experience of such generalized fear was having a shotgun trained on me from a cleaner's truck, with a police car only twenty yards away. I stood on the steps of Brown's Chapel in Selma, Alabama, in March, 1965, and I was unable to move. It is a type of experience tragically common to an increasing number of Americans. And many black American have felt it all their lives.

Pauline Kael, writing in the *New Yorker*, puts much of it

down to the anti-hero motif: "It's cool to feel that you can't win, that it's all rigged and hopeless. It's even cool to believe in purity and self-sacrifice." I saw a little of that in the deserters' vision, but there is more to it. You feel when you talk with these fellows that you are walking on water about one step out and any moment now you will all go under. And you fight that all the time. So for a moment with this film there was the illusion of instant justification by cinematic fiat—"cheap grace"—and all glory to Fonda, Hopper and Company, authors of our faith.

I remember a comment that Walter Kerr once made in a review of Rolf Hochhuth's play, *Soldiers:*

Fantasia, nightmare, unmoored fears have their own kind of authority upon occasion, the authority of the subconscious when logic lies sleeping, the authority grotesquerie assumes simply because it is more threateningly shapeless than life. Let the ground shift beneath our feet, let us feel that there *is* no ground beneath our feet, let a balloon-like face suddenly swell in the void ahead—and we attend, we worry, we do not so much think as submit.

We were struggling day by day against the submission, sometimes succumbing, often overcoming.

And so, if the American Deserters Committee in Sweden brought the war home to Americans and Swedes at the Embassy that July Fourth, *Easy Rider* hit home with something of that inner war of the human spirit that is the real battlefield for them and for all conscientious Americans these days. The ground shifts beneath our feet like some gigantic earth fault, and the command comes: "Find that solid ground, man. Find it and hold it. For yourself. For everybody." When you are "easy ridin' Amerika" there is just no other way to go.

chapter 11

UP AGAINST THE WALL, MOTHER COUNTRY

God can call in nation against nation. He can cast a damp upon any nation and make them afraid of one another. He can do an execution upon them by themselves or he can sit still in scorn, and let them melt away of themselves.

—John Donne, "How God may strike down a man to raise him up."

"As long as I can remember," Vince said, "I have had this feeling that something was wrong in America, but I thought I could get by without it affecting me. Then I began to see that things like Vietnam never happen by themselves. They happen because other things happen."

Many people are like Vince. They figure that something is terribly wrong in America but that they can get through without being hurt themselves. This is an increasingly difficult position to hold, for we are all up against it, and some of us know it. America may be hard to find, as that Catholic radical, Father Dan Berrigan, has reminded us. But when we find her, she feels amazingly like a wall.

"Dancing on the Crest of a Volcano"

On a world scale, we tremble before a tidal wave of upheaval that bids still to peak into one of history's great typhoons of social change. The United States of America, with its empire of interests around the globe run by a military-economic-ecclesiastical complex at home, has become a frightening prospect to millions of people, including many of its own. Once the country to which people turned for refuge and exile and hope, ours is now the land from which men flee for refuge. Once a nation that held out the hope of fresh starts for dissidents abroad, we now imprison our own political objectors. A person does not have to be a radical, to the right or to the left, to be aware that there is great danger in America's pursuit of its present course. As Henry James wrote prophetically in *The American Scene* this is "a society dancing all consciously on the crest of a volcano." That was in 1905. Sixty-five years later our country is up against the wall, driven there by people in the neighborhood.

As I traveled across the country for three months upon our return from Sweden, speaking along the way to many community groups, over radio and television, and to many individuals, I saw how effective the challenge of the Vietnam war deserters and resisters had been in middle America. If our crisis is anything like what I have already outlined, it is not surprising that many people should be satisfied with the dictum, "America: Love it or Leave it." Indeed, many people seem to believe that these men are, as my fellow-Episcopalian Vice-President Agnew put it, no more than "animals who belong in a zoo." A lot of people are glad that the exiles are in a "zoo"—outside America. But many other Americans, I found, also from middle America, sympathized with the deserters and resisters and in many cases openly supported their actions. If I were to guess from my experience in thirty cities over a twelve-week period, I would say that some 60 per cent were opposed while 40 per cent favored the actions of these men.

I believe that it is extremely important for all Americans to come to terms with the nature of the challenge to America that these men represent. With some understanding of the quality of their resistance, we can then proceed to talks about options for them *and* for America. Then, and only then, can we talk seriously about amnesty—what that might mean and for whom it might mean something.

A Challenge of Loyalties

The fundamental challenge that our Vietnam war resisters lay before us is to our basic loyalties as a people. The premise that America is, on balance, a force for good in the world with just demands upon its citizens to fight in its wars, to pay taxes to wage those wars and to support it when it is under attack is being questioned today as never before.

Yet it is one thing to question, and it is another thing to act on your convictions, rightly or wrongly held. American society will tolerate almost any sort of talk, so long as it does not seem to lead to anything.* For example, one fellow came around to our Solna apartment one night and we got to talking about futures: his, America's, the world's. He said with some pride, "When my son someday asks me, 'What did you do during the Vietnam war, Daddy?' you know, I'll be able to look him in the face. I'm going to say 'Son, I pulled out and I cut just a little, a very little, of the source of supply.'" Then he added, "Tom, if every one did that, really did that, I mean refused their taxes, refused induction, deserted, there wouldn't be any war in Vietnam 'cause there couldn't be." It is difficult to imagine any government permitting the course of action my young friend commended. Yet it is hard to imagine the government's policies being changed without many of its citizens following his lead.

* In one of his famous opinions (the Whitney case), Justice Louis Brandeis ruled that advocacy of action against the state is allowable "where it falls short of incitement and there is nothing to indicate that the advocacy would be immediately acted upon." The administration of *in*justice, rather than justice, has often stemmed from political judgments by those in power, which make this distinction moot in practice. For example, the conspiracy trials of the Boston Five, Drs. Spock and Coffin, and Messrs. Goodman, Ferber and Raskin and of the Chicago Eight (later Ten). While defendants in each case were alleged to have conspired to commit illegal acts against the government, none of them was finally convicted on anything more than having made speeches to certain dangerous effects. An interesting, but somewhat dated, presentation of the hierarchy of permitted speech and values in this society is found in Morton Grodzins' *The Loyal and the Disloyal* (University of Chicago Press, 1956).

"Wars will cease when men refuse to fight," it is said. Of course, this is a dream. But more and more men and women live by such a dream. James Kunen, author of *The Strawberry Statement* and far from a radical, spoke of his own experience at Columbia University during the 1968 strike.

There used to be a dream in America. . . . America was going to be different . . . free and good. Of course, they blew it right away. As soon as the Puritans came over they set up religious laws. But at least they clung to the dream. Until now. Now no one hopes for America to be different. I guess it was the dream that ruined the dream. . . . People thought the U.S.A. was special so we could do anything and it's okay. . . . I wish people would wake up and dream again.†

Some folks have. Some folks do "dream again."

It is not only the young who pick up on their hopes to dream again, convenient though that thought is to many in power. Congressman Edward I. Koch (17th C.D., Dem., New York City), for instance, returned from a visit with some of our men in Canada in January, 1970, and spoke earnestly of his impressions.

We cannot lightly dismiss these Americans because they are draft resisters and deserters. For the most part they are sensitive and mature young people who emigrated from every section of the United States. They have been outraged by our prosecution of the war in Vietnam; they have been victimized by the brutality of military training; they have been alienated by what they see as intolerance and hypocrisy in American society. . . . Those Americans who shout "America . . . love it or leave it" miss the point. The young Americans in Canada that I met nourish no hatred for their country. Neither are they cowards . . . some of them, indeed, have fought in Vietnam. . . . What they do feel is that America has deserted them by forsaking its own heritage and ideals.*

† (Random House, 1969).
* *Congressional Record*, January 21, 1970.

It would be misleading to suggest that a *conscious* moral and political idealism motivates all the men in the offending category of deserters and resisters in exile. I hope that I have made clear in earlier chapters the wondrously mixed motives that guide and sustain these young Americans. Stirred up within them, with opposition to the war and the military, are emotional deprivations from childhood, feelings of having always been used by the system or put down by it, a widespread revulsion against the phoniness of the American way of life, and a healthy dose of youthful adventurism. It seem to me that far from weakening the case of their loyalties against the claim of the United States, these complexities strengthen their case. For out of a raging sea of demands and responsibilities, they have set a course and stuck to it. They have made real choices. It is this determination that finally merits our close examination of their loyalties, and the implications of these loyalties for America. We can be freed, not threatened, by the fact that their loyalties are beyond the control of this or any other nation-state.

To understand the swing-like quality of their initial decision, the moment of their action that shapes much of their loyalty, we must remember that these men come generally from backgrounds in small-town America. Faced with hard choices, their traditionally unquestioning obedience (which led to their being considered good for soldiering in the first place) becomes its opposite number: apparent disloyalty and treason, as charged. And to reckon with this we need to be reminded that our whole history as a people is disloyal and treasonous, or was to those against whom we rebelled. The creeds of our independence in the churches are infidelities to the mother churches that birthed us and for whom we were once mission soil. Our Declaration of Independence and our Constitution were treasonous to our mother country, England, which was driven up against the wall by the resistance of our forefathers.*

* For a good, popular discussion of this fundamental problem in political experience, see Milton Mayer's *Man v. the State* (Atheneum Press, 1970; first published as an Occasional Paper by the Center for the Study of Democratic Institutions, 1969). For a general discussion of the

Paradoxically, this disloyalty to America, as understood by some, becomes a rather precise expression of the democratic ideal itself. The result is not a failure to live up to those principles that made America great. Rather, the men and women involved have had some success in living out those principles. Yet great sectors of the American public condemn these people as "misfits" or "irresponsibles." The public conveniently forgets that the Southeast Asia war is an undeclared one prosecuted by executive powers completely contrary to the express wish of the nation's founding fathers: that the Congress alone may and can declare war. Young resisters today are put down, further, for doing exactly what their government together with other Allied powers laid down as a principle at Nuremberg. Every citizen, and every soldier, is finally responsible for his actions, and can be called to account for them. Twenty-five years and several presidential wars later, the position of the United States government has shifted. Now it is more like the sign I understand was posted on a Hartford (Connecticut) exterminator's truck: "Drive Safely and Leave the Killing to Us."

I have said to the parents of our men, and I have meant it strongly that they can be proud of their sons. I believe that all Americans *could* be proud of these sons. What is needed to secure that pride, of course, is a public much more informed, and much more committed to the practice of constitutional rights and responsibilities, than the public is now. For my part I found that our young show a remarkable ability to remember and to practice, under stress, the very principles and loyalties they are alleged to deny but, in fact, have absorbed in family, in school and in the nation. As essential conservators of American tradition, they are with all their compatriots in a progressive struggle against the abuses of that tradition, our most valuable export.

---

trans-national character of what the author calls "The Great Refusal," see Theodore Roszak's *The Making of a Counter-Culture*, (Doubleday, 1969), especially chapters I and VII.

A Challenge to Families

On speaking engagements I have had people tell me in the strongest terms that I would feel differently about the Vietnam war, and not be so vehement in attacking our government's policies, there, if I knew what it felt like to have a soldier for a son or a brother. (It happens that one of my brothers is a professional soldier, a Marine and a Vietnam veteran.) What the questioners have assumed, I suppose, is that emotional ties do play a larger part in a person's rational apparatus than the proclaimers generally admit. With this I could not agree more.

But if this is so, it should work the other way when the shoe is on the other foot. When there is a resister or a deserter in your own family we can reasonably expect you to be affected. Not a few parents and families, for example, have been changed, "radicalized" if you will, by sons who said "No!" when the State ordered them to say "Yes" to induction. When it comes, however, to the men who accepted induction and then resisted, to the point of the brig or desertion, a different pattern of response emerges among the families personally involved.

On the one hand, parents of these men have often isolated their sons completely. Feelings of blood ties are suppressed. One son received from his father a one-sentence letter that commanded simply: "GET THE HELL HOME FROM THAT COMMIE ICEBERG!" There are a number of cases in my knowledge where the parents have refused all contact with their sons. Tragic though this response is, it shows how deeply ingrained is the parents' fear for their young and for themselves. It is reasonable to assume that if parents feel that way now, they probably felt similarly as they were raising their children and taught them accordingly.

On the other hand, we have seen some significant changes in the last couple of years. Until 1969 a new deserter almost never found a favorable response from his folks. Then we began to see two things happening. First, there was a process of growth for the parents of veteran deserters. More mail would come, and it would be more gentle, more concerned. Often this would be followed by the first visit.

One such reunion brought Richard, a good musician from a Jewish family in Chicago, together with his mother. Rich had been through a lot of changes in the year and a half since he had been out of the Army, part of which he had spent in Paris before he came to Sweden. He was just beginning to put a life together, which for him meant getting his music together. (He is now actively involved in a group called the "Red, White and Blues.") He told me that his mother was opening up about her feelings and that he was pleased about that. His father was having more difficulty. "This is great for my mother," Richard said. "She's pretty mixed up, you know." I smiled, apparently a little too knowingly. "No, I took Mother around to see some of the guys. We met some of them on the street and they thought she was just fabulous. So much more sensitive than their own parents. I don't know about that. But I know that she cares, she really cares. She couldn't exactly say she encouraged desertion, but now she says at least she understands why I'm here, and what I'm doing. . . . You know, she really respects me for my convictions." He was right. His mother talked about how fearful she was of making the trip, and yet how so many of her fears had passed upon seeing Richard and knowing that he was doing what he had to do.

I wish that every family of a deserter or resister in exile could have that kind of a reunion. Much of the fear that parents feel comes from ignorance. Parents, too, are often isolated by a fear of social ostracism. Sometimes they cannot discuss their son's act with even the closest of friends. The result in many homes is a crisis of emotional poverty. Rex Stout, in an early Nero Wolfe story, spoke of "the Anglo-Saxon theory of the treatment of emotions and desserts." "Freeze them and hide them in your belly," said Stout. Such repression of honest feelings is harmful and unnecessary. Each family should be encouraged, and provided with the means, to make at least one visit to its son or brother in Canada or Sweden.

We began to see another kind of reaction as well. More new

men were receiving first-round support from home. The on-goingness of the war, the increasing embitterment with the waste of it all was, I believe, settling into the American consciousness. One illustration of this was the letter from Willi's mother. Willi hails from Cheyenne, Oklahoma. He left college in his senior year at Yale, partly fed up with school and partly feeling that his II-S deferment was a cop out. He accepted I-A (O) status as a conscientious objector inside the military and ended up training fifty war dogs at Edgewood Arsenal in Maryland. When the war dogs were ordered to Vietnam, Willi was not forgotten. He made it to Sweden via New York City. His mother writes:

To many people a deserter deserves no help nor consideration—but I've dropped the word "deserter" from my vocabulary—they're just American boys confused and bothered and torn apart by too many strings pulling them. They do need help and consideration. I'm sure that each one is a different case, that the background of each is different . . . but there is a solution for each.

Bill is a wonderful son. He has never been anything but a pleasure and a joy and source of strength to his daddy and me. He was a very understanding and thoughtful child. He and I had many interests in common and my life was so happy during the time he was growing up for he included us both in much of his activity. We were older when he was born and I guess he spoiled us.

You will be happy to know that people have been so very understanding and they've reached out their arms to strengthen us. There are many things we don't understand . . . each man has his own feelings about war, etc., etc. but notwithstanding all that, our friends are concerned about us and about our son. They seem to understand that each person is trying in his own way, to do the best he can as he sees it, and that many of us are mixed up, confused, bothered and troubled. It would be unbearable if your friends turned against you in times such as these . . . but those who knew Bill and watched him grow up remember him as a good, sincere person. We talk about him with anyone who wishes to ask about him. We are proud of him and will stay by his warm side through thick or thin as he would surely do for us.

I have received a number of such letters and seen a number of such families personally. Overall, I have the impression that most parents of war resisters in exile have begun the painful process of looking at their sons as young men, no longer boys, and as a result, taking them much more seriously than ever before. The following excerpt from another mother's letter is illustrative:

People are all too prone to label them cowards, but I don't believe they concede the possibility that it also takes courage to go against all the pressures of society and family in order to do something they cannot help but feel is right.

I know that my son loves this country, and of course, me, his mother, and I must respect him for his convictions. I might also add that it has forced me to do some reevaluating of some things that I had ignored before. Apathy seems to be this country's greatest danger—also, I must add a certain blindness to facts, whether due to low intelligence or simply a noncaring attitude, I don't know. I always felt, also, that one person can do nothing to change the status quo ("You can't fight City Hall") and unfortunately you can't, alone. I love this country deeply, and it is my fervent hope that changes will come about.

A Challenge to Nationalism

One of the notes struck by the spoken and written words of the more articulate members of the exile community is that of solidarity in struggle with all people working for self-determination and freedom. Even among those not so articulate there is nonetheless a commitment to a transnational experience. Associations with German, Finnish, Japanese, Swedish and, of course, Vietnamese youth, have provided a functional equivalent to the war for many of our men.* While they remain Americans, they become de facto internationalists.

* William W., an American black, was with II Corp in South Vietnam in September, 1968. His unit was on "a sweep" where he was a loader and part-time gunner. The action was just underway when they shot

No doubt this must be their greatest offense to those Americans who feel compelled to argue "My country—right or wrong." These same people, many of whom might easily have a deserter in their own household, can come to learn the spirit of the original of that famous quotation. The editor-politician Carl Schurz (1829–1906) said it, and it is now set into a commemorative plaque in Independence Hall, Philadelphia:

> My country, right or wrong.
> When right, to keep her right.
> When wrong, to make her right.

Objectors to my appearing on radio talk shows often argued that because the actions of the men of whom I spoke were un-American, I too must be un-American and not permitted to speak. The strange logic of this position can finally do no more than isolate America from the rest of the world, even as it would bring fascism more to the surface in American life. The notion of absolute nationalism, the premise on which such charges of un-Americanism rest, is so wanting in common sense, not to say enlightened self-interest, that it is remarkable to see the hold it has upon people. Without condition, the concept of absolute sovereignty—in the nation or in individuals—is the greatest enemy of world peace today. Of course, one can justly argue, in reverse, that all who oppose such a claim by a nation may reasonably be called enemies of the State, the deserters to be counted among them.* But then, my original point is proved even as it is opposed.

---

down eight civilians under orders. The people would not leave a village. William's buddy told him, "You know, gooks, ginks, slopeheads—that's all they are." "Well," said William, "they looked like human beings to me."

* Craig Anderson, one of the Intrepid Four, spoke on Swedish Radio on his arrival: "What we believe in is reconciliation. We believe that what's poisoning the world now is ignorance. The force of ignorance is still so strong that man isn't ready to live in the technological society he's built for himself. The only thing worth doing is to try and work the ignorance out of both sides." Rick Bailey, also of the Intrepid Four, said: "We want to get away from the extreme nationalism and ideologies both East and West."

Some years ago Steve Ashton, a former student at my own alma mater, Oberlin College, went down from Oberlin, Ohio, to Hazard, Kentucky, to work with the miners there. After nearly two years of work he came out changed, bearing the open wound of America's heartland. I remember hearing about him when he came on to New York to work up some documentary material on his experiences, and to get into film generally. He said, "This country's a soul-less nation, yet there's a demand and a quest for soul—for a sense of the unity of mankind, a link. I wonder if we'll ever find it."

If we would look for any one thing we have gained from the desertion-emigration-exile pattern, which is now an expressway for the magical mystery tour of many youth, it is this sense of linkage. Perhaps this is simply a matter of going outside one's people to find oneself. Perhaps. But it is more, I think. The political nature of the act of desertion, or flight to avoid induction, and the subsequent emigration, requires deep within a man something beyond America—beyond "the American way of life"—to interpret it and to make the connections. Involvement in the life of another country, its language, its politics and its bureaucracies, even when they come down on you rather hard (perhaps especially then) can restore one's sense of soul, or help one to discover it for the first time. Again, to speak paradoxically, my identity as belonging to a particular people seems only to be confirmed by a pluralistic experience, by going up against another people, meshing with and struggling through them, for survival and for meaning.

I think, for example, of the efforts to establish a community on a farm. During the Delegation's 1968 visit, Dr. Harvey Cox of Harvard Divinity School met with Sven Kempe, a young Swede of some means who wished to help the deserters. Mr. Kempe eventually purchased a farm near the town of Torsaker, about one hundred miles north of Stockholm. Eerily isolated in a forest, some ten kilometers from the main road, the farm was leased to the American Deserters Committee and later to others who lived there communally. Sometimes the Torsaker farm became a real opportunity for men from rural backgrounds who were eager to work the land; at other times Nystilla Gard was too much of a safety valve for fellows either coming off drugs, or overly committed to their use. Over the long haul the farm went under, at least as far as our men were concerned. In fact, they blew it. Probably the main reason for this was the absence of anyone who was responsible enough to care for the farm, pay all the keep, do the work and still manage to be counselor, social worker and political guru for all the new men who kept on coming up. But there was, while it lasted, a marvelous linkage, a sense of purpose, of common struggle, of soul.

On my first visit to Torsaker, I was moved by a conversation I had with Don, a "lifer" of five and one-half years in the Army, from South Carolina. He is high school educated and his grades were good. He had joined the Army, he told me, with the idea of making it his career. Since being in Sweden, he had married. There was a child on the way. At that time he was working in the Hofors steel mill with several other fellows. "You know," he told me, "I have absolutely no compunction whatever about doing battle to defend my homeland. If by some some strange quirk of international events, the Russians decided to use Finland to come into the rest of Scandinavia and came into Sweden, I would defend my wife and home and Swedish soil, just as I would defend American soil. Thought I *was* doing that in the Army. But I finally came to the point where I could have no part of going around the world to kill and eliminate people who absolutely had done me no harm. Nor, so far as I could see, our people any harm. They [the Vietnamese] are simply no threat to the United States, to us as Americans."* Don went on to tell me how it happened that he, like the others, had refused orders to Vietnam. In his own case, he split after he had

* Nicholas von Hoffman, in a *Washington Post* column February 11, 1970, entitled "Army Doubters," has written: "It is one thing to be young and to give your life for your country and another to die for such an ugly and undefinable word as 'Vietnamization.' It has too many letters in it to be accommodated on the modest headstones of our soldiers' graves."

indicated to his superior officers that he would refuse the orders if they came down. Down they came, and off Don went.

Don's convictions illustrate the difficulty of labeling the men "deserters" or "traitors" (or "animals in a zoo") and thinking that you have dealt with them. This won't work any better than dealing with the police by calling them "pigs" or with the vice-president by calling him a "fascist." No, to understand others we must still try their shoes out for size, even if we do not, or cannot, walk in them. Try to feel, for example, the man behind the following piece from an editorial in *The Paper Grenade*. Writing for July Fourth, 1970, three years into the exile experience, the author quotes Benjamin Rush, an early American revolutionary (1787) and Wayne Hansen, a draft-card burner (1967). Then his comment follows:

The dominant theme of America may be one of ugly exploitation by the few of the many. But American history also has a strong and vigorous undercurrent—one that has opposed and resisted the forces who turned the noble experiment into a slaughterhouse of greed and racism which keeps colonies at home and maintains an empire abroad. America's radicals are conditioned to despise their country . . . to look elsewhere for their inspiration and guidance. This is because the history of the radical's "other America" or "under America" is neglected or grossly distorted beyond recognition. . . . The rulers who run our schools have convinced us that America's traditions belong to them—that radicalism and the right to revolution are foreign concepts, strangers to our shores. The words of Americans have been filled with fire and anger, with dry wit and melancholy and unconscious condemnation. Few of these words are remembered by the official "rememberers" who concoct our school books, where all men wear wigs, powder their noses and speak in platitudes.

It is time to see the other side of the American coin. The other side of the coin is not a dead one. It can be seen in the revolutionary struggle of modern America—the same struggle which we share with oppressed peoples around the world. Vietnam, Cambodia, and Laos have joined in that struggle. They are fighting valiantly to secure their independence. The peoples of Latin America and

Africa are not far behind in their search for freedom from American imperialism. . . . For July Fourth in 1970 the American revolutionary tradition gains its truth in the continuing anti-imperialist struggle led by the oppressed classes at home and abroad.

This passage, rhetorical though it sounds, is deeply felt to be one of the central paragraphs of the exiles' message to the mother country. Another paragraph was put to me by a young man of very different leanings who said, "I don't feel so much about a country now, any country. I feel a lot about people, though, all people. I think the whole world is less and less national now. At least it should be."*

The Options for America

In the parable of America today that the desertion movement has become, the point may be that when everything else seemed to be narrowing down to a few pivotal decisions—for the deserters, prison or exile as compared with continued cooperation —the choices for America had been widened out. One would have to be mad to argue on the face of it that America has many real options left. Either we will change from within, or we will be forced to change, from within or without. (Can we imagine, for example, that China will long stand for American encirclement of her borders as part of a "Pacific Rim Strategy"?) Too many people stand oppressed by either our technology or our "national interest," or more commonly, by both joined in an unholy wedlock.

At the same time, innumerable Americans have taken their lives back, to the limit of their abilities and resources, from the structures they see as having been oppressive. New options are thus opening up that were not foreseen a short time ago. I think of the decentralization of the schools and massive experimenta-

* Without pressing it, there may be an analogy between the position of the abolitionists in relation to slavery in the nineteenth century and the contemporary resistance to the involuntary servitude of conscription. *The Liberator*, magazine of the abolitionists, carried on its masthead the maxim: "The world is my country; my countrymen are all mankind."

tion in education as a prime example. If America could generally see this struggle as whole, not merely as a threat but as an opportunity, I believe that much good could flow again as life blood for our citizens, and for people around the globe. It is certain that those in power have a great deal invested in things as they are. They cannot be expected to give up power voluntarily. What is less certain is whether they will see their self-interest in change soon enough to remain in power.

Once I stood in a hospital elevator in Pittsburgh, about to visit an elderly parishioner laid up there. Scratched on the wall of that temporary prison (I don't like elevators) were the words, "I'm leaving this world. Help me to live!" Help me to live. This must surely be the cry of humanity everywhere. Today it is being uttered in desperation by millions of souls within our own borders. Is it possible that anyone anywhere is listening? Given the outside chance that those in power might realize their own stake in answering that cry, that is, their continued access to and deployment of their power, it is possible that America's answer could once again be "Yes." The right to life *is* inherent and inalienable. Like liberty. Like the pursuit of happiness. Help men to live? Yes.

Because the right to life *is* nonnegotiable, we cannot finally bargain with it. Our struggle to affirm that right does in large measure define us. Dick, a deserter now living and working in British Columbia, Canada, is an example of what I mean. Somebody asked Dick, "Who are you?" The ex-Marine said, "I haven't got that figured out yet." "Seriously, who are you?" the questioner persisted. "My name is Dick and I'm a deckhand. I'm going to be Dick the Deckhand for quite a while now." Dick the Deckhand spoke of a dream he continued to have.

There is this huge hammer and I gotta beat that freakin' hammer before it squashes me. Seems almost certain that the freakin' hammer is going to get me. That hammer in the sky, I know, is going to beat somebody in. Now I don't think that hammer is a random slash. That same hammer is used to hate niggers, only now it calls them black. I never could understand this great hammer in the sky. Why, sometimes it's made of rubber and bounces back and raps the hand behind the hammer. But that hammer, man, that hammer, it's coming down or bouncin' back ready to come down again, all the time, all the time, man.

Breathes there an American with soul so dead that he cannot see his own hand behind that hammer from time to time? So long to innocence, America. We can't claim invincible ignorance. Know-nothingism won't work anymore, especially in the guise of a new populism. Our problem now is the acceptance of guilt. Such acceptance of responsibility is the prime spiritual condition for actually receiving pardon. There are writers who believe that after Vietnam nothing short of a second Nuremberg—this time with America on the receiving end—will bring America to its senses. There are indications that we have begun already to do some guilt-finding. Unhappily, we are looking for scapegoats. Hence the numerous indictments of enlisted men, and only a few officers, for the My Lai massacre. Hence the trials of political dissidents. Hence the legal lynchings of groups like the Black Panther party. Thus far, such guilt-finding misses the mark, for it seeks a few individuals or groups to take responsibility for wrongs in which we all, in varying ways, participate.

How, then, do people take corporate responsibility? After all, we the people have been the taxpayers for this war, and we the people have surrendered our sons and brothers, all without much more resistance than a grumble. How then can we begin to shake loose the demoniacal prospect of scapegoating and blood-letting for our crimes of cooperation? Seymour Hersh said of his Dispatch News Agency's unfolding of the My Lai story, "What we did was to surface the cancerous fingernail of the war in Vietnam." What if it turns out that we *are* a cancer-ridden society, infected with our own brand of messianism, that communicable disease for which we are now the chief, but by no means the only, carrier on the earth? What if, at the autopsy of America, Martin Luther King, Jr., is proved right when he said: "America is the greatest purveyor of violence in the world today?" That is to say, how can the blind lead the blind, or the lame heal the lame?

On speaking in Chicago, as the judgment was brought in on the Chicago Conspiracy Trial, I was asked what I thought of the vice-president's remarks about the deserters and resisters ("animals in a zoo," remember?) I said—more angrily than flippantly—that he was like a man dying of cancer with no one in the family, not even the family doctor, to tell him the truth. That is far more true of our society as a whole. I doubt if any of us can say that the process is irreversible. We must act in the conviction that it is not, that the cancer can be exorcised. But let us not mistake that the operation is serious, and the patient is in a critical condition.

What is clearly needed is the corporate, general and widespread admission that Vietnam was not a historical accident, something we just "fell into," but a moral fault and a political sin. I believe that unless we go that deep and admit that we were and are in a state of moral and spiritual error, our political adjustments will be merely that: adjustment, not change.*

Amnesty? For whom?

It is surely a sign of the impact the deserters and resisters have had upon us that the issue of amnesty for them has al-

---

* Though total troop withdrawals from Vietnam would be seen by most of the citizenry as an end to the Vietnam war, there is yet another prospect. Counter-insurgency "fire brigades" are being readied by the U.S., with highly advanced air technology, which would enable us to intervene in Southeast Asia even if all troops were withdrawn. Defense Secretary Melvin Laird has indicated that several thousand "advisory personnel" would remain in Vietnam after the fighting ended in any case. For development of this thesis see Michael Klare's ominous pre-Cambodia article, "The Great South Asian War," *The Nation*, March 9, 1970.

Also a July 12, 1970, story by Neil Sheehan in *The New York Times* referred to "knowledgeable military sources" in Washington who project that 150,000 to 200,000 Americans would be needed to bolster the Saigon regime as late as 1972. According to Sheehan, "The implication of this military assessment is that President Nixon may well have to face the electorate in 1972 with a sizeable war still under way in Vietnam and significant numbers of American casualties. . . ."

ready been widely advanced, and condemned, well before the United States has withdrawn its forces from Southeast Asia. As might be expected, the favorable arguments have come from America's religious community, notably from the efforts of Clergy and Laymen Concerned about Vietnam.

In a pamphlet originally published in the *National Catholic Reporter*,* Methodist theologian Dr. John M. Swomley, Jr., argued that "the test of how democratic any government is depends upon the number of political prisoners it keeps behind bars. . . . The United States' reputation as a democracy would be enhanced rather than diminished by amnesty for those who are in prisons for draft-related offenses as well as for those who are in exile or still awaiting trial." Pastor Richard John Neuhaus, sometime candidate for the U.S. Congress, pastor of St. John the Evangelist Church in Brooklyn and one of the founders of CALCAV, reasons that amnesty is really part of the legal process: "[a] legal instrument in those instances where it is thought that magnanimity will serve the society's interests better than punishment." He adds that amnesty, as distinguished from pardon (which "forgives" the wrong of the State toward the individual), makes "good sense." To this effect, pragmatic politicians in the United States Senate have prepared bills and stand ready to introduce them at "a propitious time."

The proposal for an amnesty toward the general category of draft and Vietnam military service offenders is being taken seriously in many quarters. Thousands of citizens have signed petitions calling for it. Letters to the editors of local newspapers show that the issue is a lively one. And no less an analyst that Tom Wicker of the Washington bureau of *The New York Times* brought the question of amnesty to the fore in a column written early in the Nixon administration.† ". . . The contention

---

* *Amnesty: The Record and the Need.* CALCAV, 637 West 125th St., New York, N.Y. 10027 (20 cents). An essential introduction to this issue.

† February 13, 1969.

that amnesty would foster greater disrespect for the conscription law runs afoul of Mr. Nixon's own criticism of that law and his repeated pledges to abolish it and provide a volunteer army," wrote Mr. Wicker. "It is not true, moreover," he added, "that amnestied youths will have paid no price. To stand on moral ground against the general view is never easy; physical exile is a haunting personal situation. . . ."

I confess to some misgivings about the whole procedure of the debate on amnesty thus far. Until now it has been argued by the other side in the question that "they paid their money and they made their choice," as Mr. Wicker himself noted. Somehow I think this position is more honest than what may well turn out to be the greatest engineering feat in history: Mr. Nixon's bridge over the generation gap. If that bridge is ever built, it is likely to include amnesty for resisters as one of its pillars. Presuming that Mr. Nixon does withdraw troops in "sufficient" numbers, with a "sufficient" decrease in American casualties, it is not unlikely that he might announce, prior to the 1972 elections, that he promises amnesty to those in prison and in exile abroad, "subject, of course, to safeguards to our national security." That is to say, amnesty for our Vietnam war resisters may ironically turn out to be accompanied by the self-indulgent pardon of the executive branch of government, which prosecuted the war.

Andrew Johnson proclaimed executive amnesties in 1865, 1867 and on July Fourth, 1868, to those who "participated in the late insurrection or rebellion." On December 25, 1868, amnesty was granted even to those who had committed "the offense of treason against the United States." Thus, for a previous president even treason could be amnestied. Without judging motives, it is clear that President Johnson at that time needed unity to govern, and paid a price to get it. Another president, one who campaigned "to bring us together again," might resort to a similar gesture. It is doubtful, however, that the president would move toward amnesty without the pressure and support of public opinion.

The public debate on the question is not without humor, as one can tell from reading newspaper editorials on the subject. The New York *Daily News* attacked Congressman Koch, for example, when he returned from his visit to Canada and proposed, as an addendum to his report, that amnesty should be granted. The deserters, said the *Daily News*, were "a sorry lot, to be pitied, not pardoned." The *Chicago Tribune* said "[they] are not barred from America. They can return whenever they want, so long as they are prepared to pay the penalty for their moral poltroonery."* Such comments conjure in my mind the professional pity of some funeral directors I have known.

Let us underscore our point. The deserters and the resisters, in exile or in prison, may not be ridiculed on the conservative's block of scorn, or pitied by the liberal's cup of tears. Not, that is, if the war objectors are to be taken seriously as human beings. I take some satisfaction from knowing that our men in Fort Leavenworth and in Allenwood and in Stockholm and in Toronto will outlive every attempt to put them down, and outgrow every category used to write them off. Simply put, they are human beings who have committed a political act in relation to an undeclared war, an act that requires a political response, whether one agrees with their action or not.

The question, then, is amnesty for whom? For all who have resisted induction only, and accepted imprisonment? For those who have avoided induction as well? (General Hershey would then have to be amnestied for encouraging draft dodging, the selective service system has had so many loopholes.) For those who refused orders, or disobeyed orders to Vietnam, among them thousands of the 25,000 GI's now in our stockades? For the deserters gone AWOL more than thirty days? More than six months? What of the apparent conflicts between military and civilian jurisdictions? Could "military justice" be trusted to come into play even with a presidential amnesty? What of the

---

* Whatever "poltoonery" is. Most etymologists believe its origin is in the Latin, *pullus*, for a young animal; hence adolescence, idleness. I suppose the editorial writer means "moral truancy."

effect of amnesty upon Vietnam veterans and their families? Would they not feel morally and politically short-changed? Finally, do not the answers to these questions involve a political judgment of our own as to the moral rightness and political wisdom of the United States' prosecution of the Southeast Asian war? Who amnesties whom? These are questions that would be idle to ask if we had the answers. But they suggest, I hope, that large numbers of Americans have a stake in the answers. Indeed, these are questions we all need to do a great deal of pondering about.

There was an unheralded amnesty of military deserters as recently as the Korean conflict, for those men who had not fled the Korean battlefield but did desert from the armed forces at that time. (I ran across one potential recipient of that decision. He turned down the chance to return to the United States, and is now teaching in the University of Stockholm.) The mechanics involved, after all, are part of our history from the founding of the republic until now. If we flounder on procedures it will be because we are eager to do so. For the exiles themselves, it is increasingly only a matter of curiosity whether an amnesty shall ever be granted. They do not sit pining away on the issue, nor do they consider amnesty likely. The longer the war is waged (we are now into our third decade in Southeast Asia, where we began by supporting the French in 1949) the less likely these men are to think in terms of America at all. This, I believe, is our greatest loss—the real chance that *we* shall not have them back, not to speak of the loss for their families and friends. I cannot imagine those who know the exiles being callous about the possibilities for their eventual return. For I am convinced of the enormous contribution these men can make to building the new America from the ashes of our present conflagrations.

This latter note was implicit in the significant statement of the late Richard Cardinal Cushing of the Roman Catholic Archdiocese of Boston on Easter Even, March 28, 1970. The Cardinal said:

Perhaps this year we should dramatize this notion of beginning, of newness, by doing something unprecedented in our life as a nation. These are troubled times, we know—times that in another age would have been called "out of joint." . . .

[The deserters and resisters] are bewildered, confused protesters against a world they are reluctant to inherit. They seek beauty but find it only in rags and drugs. They search for love and all they find is sex. So very badly they need the new life of which we have been speaking, so desperately they are driven that they should have the chance to make a new beginning.

The Cardinal then called for a presidential amnesty for those in prison and in exile for their resistance to the Vietnam war. His view of today's youth was more than a little patronizing, of course, but the note of new beginnings is nevertheless a vital one, not to be lost in the debate about the politics of amnesty.

We got into a discussion of the question of amnesty one night in Stockholm, and one fellow quite vehemently denounced any proposals toward amnesty whatsoever. "Amnesty? I wouldn't accept it if they offered it to me, 'cause I haven't done anything wrong. In fact, to accept it would be to agree with them. If *they* want amnesty for us that's their business, not ours." I submit that it is *our* business whether or not the men in exile are interested, and whether or not we happen to agree with their actions. In the end, those who do return may find that they are in exile, or feel that way, in their own land.* Be that as it may, the opportunity is there for us as a nation, for us, "the people," to *come to terms with ourselves*, with our guilt for the prosecution of the war, with our repression by consent at home, and with our hope for a newer, truer America.

* Some readers may have seen the *Look* magazine story by Richard Gooding, "An exile in my own country . . .", February 24, 1970. Gooding refused induction and, instead of going to prison or into exile, decided to try to live underground. Peter Collier's *Ramparts* article, February, 1970, "The Unilateral Withdrawal of Private Weise," tells the story of David Weise who lived underground for fourteen months before going to Canada in December, 1969. Both articles are remarkably insightful statements of how America feels from its "underbelly."

In the last analysis, it is, after all, mother country that is up against it, not our war resisters. Our men in exile, our war objectors in prison, have gotten it together and can take care of themselves. The question they pose, the challenge that sends us up against the wall is whether we, their parents, the elders of America, have done as much or as well in trying to end the madness of war.

chapter 12

OLD DESERT: NEW EXODUS

Like these good figs, so I will regard as good the exiles
from Judah, whom I have sent away from this place to the
land of the Chaldeans. . . . [The bad figs] I will make . . .
a horror to all the kingdoms of the earth, to be a reproach,
a byword, a taunt, and a curse in all the places where I
shall drive them.

Build houses and live in them; plant gardens and eat their
produce . . . multiply there. . . . But seek the welfare of the
city where I have sent you into exile, and pray to the
Lord on its behalf, for in its welfare you will find your welfare. . . . When seventy years are completed for Babylon,
I will visit you . . . and bring you back. . . . I know the plans
I have for you . . . plans for welfare and not for evil, to give
you a future and a hope.

—Jeremiah 24, 29; on Nebuchadrezzar's taking
the Jews from Jerusalem to Babylon, 597–586 B.C.

Jeremiah's seventy years is a long time in exile, indeed. It is
not, however, without precedent or sequel. Those men and
women who today embark upon a new exodus—voluntary or
imposed—move into every bit as uncertain a future as their
most honorable predecessors of many nations, tongues and
circumstances.

What they may be up against, though, is something qualita-
tively different from anything their ancestors have known.
Nobel Laureate and Harvard professor Dr. George Wald noted
in his now-famous March Fourth (1969) speech that this gen-

178

eration is "by no means certain that it has a future." Jeremiah
could reasonably prophesy that the world would go on, that
history would unfold and that God would work his good purposes out in due time. The people whom the prophet Jeremiah
loved were promised "a future and a hope." We are not so sure.

We need to examine these accepted truths to see whether
there is any prospect of a future and any presence of hope. Before we do this, however, we must deal with a potentially destructive reality in our experience now: it is very difficult to be
a civilian in a world of soldiers.

Thinking Civilian

In our day it's almost a crime to be a civilian. We are all
conscripts of some nation, ideology or belief. To dissent, to
oppose, especially to set one's own body directly in the path of
the all-powerful rule of government is to ask for the first plane
out or for the first open cell. I remember sitting in a room in
Uppsala, Sweden, where a Christian socialist community dis-
cussed its concerns and proposals. In walked a young Finnish
fellow wearing a well-inked T-shirt. He had marked himself
with the words, "I AM AN OUTCAST. HAVE MERCY
PLEASE." He simply asserted what was fact from many of
those present. By the various associations of their existence, they
were outside the ordinary bounds of social conduct. That is, by
noncooperation with the contemporary powers that be they were
beyond managerial control. Together, they were the model of
what it is to be civilian in a world where everything and everyone is marshalled to the command of something or someone
else. Some, in fact, had served prison sentences for draft refusal and political protest of one sort or another. Their vocation
was to become civilians in a city not yet on the drawing board
of any of the world's urban planners.

Trying to become a civilian, when one is clearly supposed to
be a conscript, has to be one of the most dangerous adventures
of the human species. In October, 1966, *The New York Times*
carried a revealing story about two German sailors who were

executed five days after the end of World War II. Bruno Dorfer and Ranier Beck were killed in Holland on May 13, 1945, with the consent of Canadian military authorities to whom they had fled for sanctuary. Beck's family (he was 28 in 1945) reopened the case and the story was broken by *Der Spiegel*. Dorfer was younger, at 20. A public prosecutor for the city of Cologne represented Ranier Beck's family.

Beck and Dorfer jumped ship and went into hiding until V-E day when they surrendered to the Canadians and were sent to a Canadian camp in the Netherlands. Turned over to their German superiors by the Canadians, the two would-be civilians were then court-martialed and killed inside the camp by a German firing squad.

The German who was the chief officer in the court-martial claimed that "the whole affair was organized by the Canadian commander." "They even decided where to hold the execution," he added. A representative of the Canadian embassy in Bonn argued, on the other hand, that because the camp held only surrendered troops and not prisoners of war, "Canadian military authorities did not have jurisdiction over those troops. They [the Germans] were responsible for their own affairs."

Clearly, the Canadian diplomat meant to imply that the German officers had control of the situation, command over their own men, and that the Canadian commander should be exonerated from any wrongdoing as he "had no jurisdiction."

What is remarkable about the story—and so worth Americans remembering—is the contradiction between the image of the "good Canadians" who pleaded for observance of the "Nuremberg principle" (in the trials of German war criminals after the war), and their easy justification years later of fraternal cooperation between the two sets of top brass who were otherwise "enemies." Beck's and Dorfer's desertions come down to us as penultimate acts of subverting militarism, to be succeeded only by burying war itself.

The victorious Canadians had so little sympathy for Beck and Dorfer that one imagines, with the tables turned around, the Germans would have extended the same "military courtesy" to the Canadians. In the exchange that took the lives of these ex-sailors of another day and time, we see how expendable civilians, actual or potential, are to the machinery of war.

It is not simply the following or disobeying of orders that must be judged with discretion; the universal right to life of all human creatures must be made preeminent. In the perspective of that hope against hope, how much difference is there between Guernica and Dresden, between Dachau and Hiroshima? The horrendous crime in the midst of war is to be a civilian, making the claims of a civilian and calling men to peace again.

Trying to become or remain a civilian in the jaws of the monster of modern war may be considered by some who exercise power to be a crime punishable by death. No journey toward any future for modern man can ignore this fact. If we continue to follow the generals of the world, we will commit ecocide and destroy the whole earth household. We must consider our adherence to war, both the practice and the preparations for it, to be a crime against our own humanity, the most desperate kind of self-hate. Otherwise I do not see how any of us can speak of hope, of peace, of any future at all.

We change the possibilities for man by the way we imagine ourselves, and we simply have not considered in any depth our vocation to be civilians. We have so let ourselves be defined by soldiery, recruitment in causes and enterprises of all kinds, that most of us are described negatively in history books as "noncombatants." That the human species has a struggle defined more by the attempt to be human than by battles against others of the same species seems seldom to occur to even the most thoughtful of men.

We have let pass for an authentic condition of our personhood the *illusion* that we are civilians, thereby surrendering ourselves to the marching orders of others. It is interesting to note how this civilian-soldier role tension works out in the mind of the professional soldier as well. A group of West Point cadets were experiencing such isolation from the civilian population that they went to their chaplain and asked him to arrange for a retreat with students and others from the New York area. The resulting exchange illuminated the feelings troubling the cadets. Challenged as to their acceptance of their roles as officers for the U.S. military establishment, they confessed to feeling felt very much like outcasts in civilian society. At home, they were ignored or put down by their peers. Their parents could not comprehend what it felt like for their sons to see West Point as "the pipe" or "the funnel" draining out at least the next ten years of their lives.

When the cadets were pressed about their convictions on the war, they responded in a significant fashion. "It is the civilian's role to make policy; we merely implement what the civilian sector requires," one said. The judgments of Nuremberg were raised and the cadets accounted themselves responsible for observing the Uniform Code of Military Justice and for saving as many lives of their men as possible. The rest was up to "the civilian sector."

Perhaps if the cadets had not felt so much on the defensive, they might have asked the civilians present to what extent they were indeed civilians. Most of the students and adults there were against the war in varying ways. In fact, however, few had involved themselves to any extent in "clogging with their whole weight." They were as content to be conscripts or recruits for the established war policies as the cadets. At least the cadets were honest in their professionalism.

If we are going to be civilians, we had better get serious about thinking civilian. The way you see it makes the difference, as those disturbed cadets show us. If you keep on looking at the world through a keyhole, pretty soon the world is keyhole shaped. This is self-defeating if your goal is to make the earth household livable for humanness. You never get beyond the door when you are on your knees and only sneaking a peek at the room inside.

There is a handicap to our ever getting underway. Jan Myrdal calls it "the Life Lie," the addiction to commonplace untruths in our culture.* We seem to suffer from moral paraplegia, the result of an apparently permanent injury to the spine of the human conscience. This disease is so widespread that when something goes wrong, our first response is commonly, "Why doesn't somebody do something about that?" I understand that physical paraplegics have become so adept with their wheelchairs that an international "parathletics" games has been planned. Those of us more fortunate by birth could well take an advanced course in fortitude from these people. When taking things into your own hands is considered, arbitrarily, a bad thing to do, something fundamental is wrong within us. One mark of our vocation as civilian is surely that we recognize this complacency as a handicap and begin to overcome it. We cannot continue to have all the advantages of life without real choosing between risks. Leon Blum once said, in discussing marriage: "I have often thought that morality may perhaps consist solely in the courage of making a choice."

Growing Up on the Way

Our ministry in Sweden was parabolic of the commitment we make generally. In our time, the church's ministry, not to mention the whole human enterprise, is an Exodus ministry, a maturing under pressure, a reaching out for liberation, "roadwork." Which is to say that we grow as we go. And only so. This gift of growth among the deserters and resisters themselves was undoubtedly the most exciting grant made to us during our time in Sweden, and it continues to be our reward.

It happened something like this. A great rain-wind storm came to both coasts of Sweden in the fall of that year. In the

---

* "In order not to hurt people, I have to tamper with my insight. Already as a child you are told that there are truths you had better keep for yourself. But it is inconvenient to falsify yourself to suit others. You become an addict. Illusions are like narcotics. In utilizing the commonplace lies of our culture you will soon find that you can't live without them. The life lie. The breaking of this habit is painful." *Confessions of a Disloyal European* (Random House, 1968), p. 165.

west, around Gothenburg, human lives were lost. In the east, around Stockholm, it was not so devastating. Yet the trees were uprooted so that their roots faced out toward us as if to stare us down. We learned that these trees could be replanted within a short period of time and live. Some of the trees, it being near to winter, were able to survive the snows as long as they had sufficient soil clothing the exposed roots.

Our men, like those trees, are managing to survive a life-changing uprooting. For each of them, it is not too much to suggest that in their act of desertion there is the power of death itself. In all but a few cases (those are our "paralyzed ones"), the men manage to have enough emotional soil and enough outside help from others in their midst to plant themselves and to begin to grow new roots.

I used to think of time-lapse photography as I saw the fellows grow. From week to week, they would develop so fast that their lives seemed foreshortened somehow. You know that process of photography, in which the blooming of flowers can be shown to occur before your eyes. What takes weeks or even a year can be suggested in minutes.

One fellow in particular came to town in August from Southern California. Andy was about twenty, and as naive a young man as I have ever met. It developed that Andy's father, an Army colonel, had sent him to Sweden—Andy said, "to make a man out of me." His father must be a master judge of men to know his own son so well. Inside two months, Andy had taken responsibility for his life in a way I could not believe. He had begun to get his language down, begun to relate to others and, above all, begun to gain a sense of humor. He had not laughed at himself, though I could hardly hold my sides in, when he told us of his father's command. Later we learned that Andy genuinely abhorred the prospect of being a soldier, that his father understood this and, in fact, sympathized with his son (his mother less so), and had quietly suggested that Andy emigrate abroad as his way of growing up.

I think there are situations in human experience, when we

come very close to knowing that we are, as our language accurately puts it, "dead-ended." One's own death is hinted at, at least the prospect of having done everything with any meaning that one is going to do. We personally came to that point in our work in Stockholm. In order for the men to embrace a future that, after all, was theirs, I felt that my mission was to work myself out of a job. That mission was a painful one for me and for all the Hayeses. In a relatively brief span of time our lives had become bound up with theirs. What happened to them happened to us, and for some of them it worked the other way around as well.

One key factor in this decision was the realization that a sizable number of men had come to depend upon me, upon my wife, Janet, upon our family of four, Sharon and Jennifer included, in what was a "down-home syndrome." We became a retreat house, from which some fellows found it difficult to advance. There was for some an illusion of security, one that did not derive from within the self but from outside. I foresaw this as potentially destructive for the persons involved and for the body politic as a whole. Whatever the Hayeses had been able to do had been done. Further efforts would probably result in little more than deepened personal attachments, a development that I felt could be divisive. We spent nearly four months preparing individuals for our departure. After consulting with men representing a number of points of view we concluded that the time had come for our support to be continued from our home base in the States.

The shape of their future in Sweden has become clearer as a result of several developments since our return. The first, a negative force, was the arrest in early 1970 of several men on drug charges. One arrest, widely reported in the American press, originally alleged that ten deserters had been involved in an LSD smuggling ring. In fact, three were so charged. This affected me personally quite deeply, as I knew two of the men well. Jim, a twenty-two-year-old Afro-American, had told me and some of his buddies the August before when we were into plans for a folk-rock group, "I spent last winter in the cold, and out on the streets, and I'm asking you are you serious. I'm telling you right now I'm not going to do that again this year." In the Swedish press, the deserters began to be pictured for the first time as being responsible for drug traffic in Sweden. Without going into the long debate within Swedish life on this question, it is enough to say there has been, and is now, in Sweden a drug hysteria without sufficient understanding or medical help being made available to meet the problems. It is not unlike the situation in the United States.

The effect on the American exiles was positive, however. A good deal of their work has been related to incoming men. In addition, a number of people began to meet to see what could be tried in dealing with the drug problems. The outcome of this is The Center, a storefront operation on Gotlandsgatan 73. With the help of a national organization for help for drug abuses, both ADC and non-ADC members have joined together in a common effort to make contact with fellows on the streets, and to develop methods for finding jobs and housing. The Center is seen as a kind of middle-man (their word) between those in need and those who can help. About a dozen Americans, plus their Swedish wives or girlfriends, are working on this project.

So the men continue to plod through an old desert on the New Exodus. We have said the decisive shape of their future is exodic: going out from the familiar and known, going out of necessity into the strange and frightening unknown. What we have not made very clear is that as they embark the promise of a future is felt to be real. Where it may lead is unknown. How long it may last is beyond comprehension. But, for them, the future is already here.

The deserter, for example, knows by the nature of his act (or he is driven to know it after the fact) that his future is built into the present course of his life. His decision comes up to meet him from the day he splits. It does not surface from his past. It comes at him from his future. Mike C., folksinger and

deserter, enjoyed singing an old blues tune by Willie Brown
whose words go:

> I don't know my future, baby,
> and I sure ain't gonna tell my past.
> You know, it seems like any minute now
> is gonna be my last.

Jean-Luc Godard catches this in a phrase in an early film
when on the soundtrack he describes as his own field of work
"the present, where the future is more present than the present."
I do not see any other way of interpreting that most significant
of characteristics about our men in Sweden, namely, that there
was so little looking back, and no regret for the act of desertion.
How explain this unless there is a secret "futurable" built into
the risk taken, the life conceived, the conscience obeyed? Surely
if such decisions were not very deep within the men, there
would be regression and self-pity in great abundance. But that
does not seem to be the case.

Jewish Talmudic tradition has it that after Jerusalem's Second Temple fell, people were no longer considered worthy of
the gift of prophecy. Yet, it was argued by the rabbis, how
could people survive were God to deny to the universe the
presence of his prophets? So it came to be believed that God
was an ingenuous strategist. He had a contingency plan. The
gift of prophecy—reading the times—would be given only to
children and to fools. Thus the gift was to be rendered indistinguishable from their other utterances. The rabbis reasoned
that the prophetic gift would be well entrusted and quite secure
for posterity.

Is it not possible that we can reclaim that gift and read the
times ourselves by "suffering fools gladly?" Those who seem
most insane when all other men claim to be reasonable may
turn out to be the reasonable ones, after all. I remember a letter
my wife received from a college classmate as we were about to
leave for Sweden. "I think what you and your husband are

doing is wonderful," she wrote. "I hope they all come to their senses and stand behind the United States." What if, on balance those thousands in the New Exodus are of sound mind and *have* come to their senses? What if they are out in front of America, widening the options for themselves, and in the process, challenging us to rediscover our own roots? What then? Shall we not at least consider that a word of risk and hope is given to us in the lives of these radical decision-makers? Perhaps our own future is present with them and theirs with us in a way yet to be revealed, but certain enough now to be trusted.

The Presence of Hope

The secret of a kingdom of hope is within us. We are not without help as we walk the road of the New Exodus. In order for us, however, to appropriate that help we have to learn how to make despair work for us, and not against us.

A great deal more is required of us in emigrating to a workable future than merely the crossing of national or social boundaries. No sooner do we seek to dig into another life style, to risk a new commitment, than we recognize our old, familiar selves. Thinking that a new place or another neighborhood might solve our problems, we may be quite frightened to discover that we remain captives of our past. Deserters and resisters who have exchanged Canada for Sweden, or the reverse, have soon learned that their situation is not fundamentally altered. Stories abound that suggest otherwise, that in one or another country "you have it made," but it just isn't so.

Whatever your mental geography is, wherever you find yourself in the New Exodus, there are reminders that this is a journey without maps and only a few signs. One such sign I remember seeing in a telephone booth of an apartment house in Toronto, where a number of exiles had been living. As in all such pads, it became necessary to control the use of the phone. Over the wall was scribbled a command, "No Long Distance Calls." And in another hand someone had added, "Don't look back."

"Don't look back" is more than casual counsel. (I have seen some telephone bills run into hundreds of dollars.) It is a warning of psychic danger for anyone who has split for good. There are going to be casualties every time someone is caught between the terrible struggle of his present search and the felt security— illusory or not—of his past.

Jesus, an early organizer of the New Exodus, reminded us of what we need to know. To the man who wanted first to say goodbye to his family before he set out with him, Jesus said, "No one who sets his hand to the plow and then keeps looking back is fit for the kingdom of God." Once we have set our sight, and made our move, there can be no looking back. The temptation to return, to avoid the risk of failure, is enormous. Looking back over your shoulder can be fatal to the struggle. Finally, one has to put together an analysis of his situation that makes sense out of the sacrifice, and in due time begins to gather in its own reward of freshness and hope.

It is doubtful that those who do not learn how to do this—to make a sacrament of their despair—will ever make it to the Promised Land. Within us there is more hope than we have yet tapped. And it is our own existential experience—what actually happens to us combined with what we make happen— that is our strongest weapon. ALL POWER TO THE PEOPLE is quite literally true for pilgrims of the New Exodus. You can't eat a slogan, or sleep on a poster.

Yet it is absurd to tell someone that all that pain, that struggle, that migration from home, that moving around abroad in the earth, and that thunderous fear that all will come to naught is *good* for him! That is like telling a young man he should join the Army because it will "make a man outa you." No, it is much simpler than such moralizing, and much truer. For the freedom of a person today it is necessary above all that he take his own *potentiality* to be free more seriously than he ever dreamed. He or she will soon discover that you can't be free by yourself, that you can't be truly human alone. But to learn that, you have to live it, and no one else can do that for you. Unless you have gone through something like the New

Exodus decision you cannot imagine the taste of victory for the human spirit that comes from making that despair work for you. All the things that terrorize you, often suddenly when you thought you had it "together," somehow become sacramental. The reality trip begins to feel like a holy thing and you desire to pay homage to "it." In the process, "it" becomes "thou."

Feeling the pain and sharing the loss seem inescapable. I remember Bob S., who died a suicide. He knew what he had to do, but he was overwhelmed and couldn't do it. I remember Greg V., who died in a drowning accident. He knew what he had to do and was not given the time to do it. I remember Jimmy D., who knew what he had to do, too, but was caught trying to make it another way. I think of Bob and Greg and Jimmy as casualties of peace. The suffering for those who know these men is different in each case; but taken together, we who knew them are caught up anew in the things that make for their peace, our peace.

More than the suffering, however, a malaise of spirit hangs over America like a cloud of polluted air. Hundreds of thousands of words pour out but nothing significant seems to happen. A toll is taken in fractured lives, marriages and relationships among those who have gone up against The Wall. And I don't imagine it is much different for those people, not in "the Movement," who are simply "out there" somewhere.

Among our Vietnam war resisters in prison and in exile this sense of malaise is compounded by the feeling that their own country has become one of history's nightmares. The feeling overtakes you like a spiritual plague. If you are abroad in Europe you may read the *International Herald Tribune*. When you discover that every day half of that paper is devoted to America's international banking interests, you try to ward off "the sickness." Only there is no quarantine. The disease seems to move faster than the human spirit can deal with. Every American is infected with it in one form or another. And when an individual is isolated from his fellows in struggle, the vulnerability increases many times over and a spiritual death is almost certain. Temporary paralysis of the self is common. The withdrawal of middle America even finds its occasional counterpart in withdrawal among the exiles. It seems that many people have simply "had it."

What we have seen among our exiles, therefore, is profoundly sacramental. All the profaneness of the old desert of the human struggle is being turned right side up by the presence of a real hope, one that anticipates but does not depend upon their eventual vindication. That conviction is finally special with each young man or woman precisely because it is required that each one know that he or she *is* the struggle, not merely *in* it. It is to know that what we do, or fail to do, after all, does make a difference.

These, then, are some of the people, some of the demands and some of the hopes that are driving America, still the mother country for millions, up against the wall in the 1970's. I believe I have shown that this is not a bad thing, that the wall beyond which we cannot go really is transcendent humanness, and that there is, indeed, a revolutionary hope as deeply driven into the American spirit as a steel piling.

Thoreau once referred to soldiers as "a movable fort." Perhaps it is so. But aren't we all? We *are* our message. We are, finally, what we stand for. The great gift of the desertion movement is to bring that home to us with the clarity of a mountain stream, to be parabolic of the new Exodus through which the progressive movement of people must pass on the way to a new America.

Galway Kinnell, one of our more sensitive younger poets, expresses this powerfully in "Another Night in the Ruins."*

> How many nights must it take
> one such as me to learn
> that we aren't, after all, made
> from that bird which flies out of its ashes,
> that for a man

* From *Body Rags* by Galway Kinnell (Boston: Houghton Mifflin Co., 1968).

as he goes up in flames, his one work
is
to open himself, to be
the flames?

In other words, suppose they gave a war, and right in the middle of it a lot of people left for good?